WHILE WE WAIT

Advance Praise for
WHILE WE WAIT

❦ ❦ ❦

This book is an honest, compassionate, and encouraging spiritual resource. I learned so much from Heidi's Schlumpf's insights and her lived experience as an adoptive parent.

— Joyce Rupp
author of *God's Enduring Presence*

❦ ❦ ❦

While We Wait *is a candid and heartfelt account of the emotional journey prospective parents travel when building their families through adoption. Heidi Schlumpf's message is both affirming and inspiring as she speaks to the many struggles encountered along the path to parenthood. Her words—coupled with the writings of beloved spiritual leaders—are a true gift of hope to those who wait.*

— Therese Bartlett
author of *When You Were Born in Vietnam*
and Hague Convention Adoption Specialist,
Lutheran Social Service of Minnesota

WHILE WE WAIT

Spiritual & Practical Advice
for Those Trying to Adopt

Heidi Schlumpf

PUBLICATIONS

WHILE WE WAIT
Spiritual & Practical Advice for Those Waiting to Adopt
Heidi Schlumpf

Edited by Andrew Yankech
Cover design by Tom A. Wright
Text Design and typesetting by Patricia A. Lynch

Scripture quotations are from the *New Revised Standard Version Bible*, copyright ©
1989 by the Division of Christian Education of the National Council of the Churches of Christ in the USA. Used by permission. All rights reserved.

Copyright © 2009 by Heidi Schlumpf

Published by ACTA Publications, 5559 W. Howard Street, Skokie, IL 60077-2621,
(800) 397-2282, www.actapublications.com

Library of Congress Number: 2009930512
ISBN: 978-0-87946-406-6
Printed in The United States by Versa Press
Year 16 15 14 13 12 11 10 09
Printing 10 09 08 07 06 05 04 03 02 First Edition

♻ Printed on 30% post-consumer waste recycled paper

CONTENTS

Not Alone: Those Who Wait With Us

When the Going Gets Tough

Coping Strategies

Spiritual Resources

Epilogue

To Edmund,
who waited with me.

❧

In gratitude to all who supported us while we waited: our families, our friends, our co-workers. Thanks to Greg Pierce at ACTA Publications for suggesting that I share my reflections about our wait through this book, and to Andrew Yankech for his excellent editing. Special thanks to those who read and improved upon the original manuscript: Amy Schlumpf Manion, Karen Radtke, Dr. Kristin Kenefick, and Bryan Cones. Finally, to all those who helped facilitate our adoptions and, most importantly, to our children's birthparents—who gave us something worth waiting for.

INTRODUCTION

I t was supposed to be a nice, simple afternoon in the park. But as my husband, Edmund, and I moved into the second year of waiting for our adopted child, everything—even a simple afternoon in the park—was turning into a spiritual lesson on the art of waiting.

When we heard that the Dalai Lama, whom Tibetan Buddhists believe is the reincarnation of the Buddha, was coming to Chicago, Edmund and I were both interested in his free public talk on "Finding Inner Peace in Turmoil." After all, between our own career woes and our continuing adoption saga, we had plenty of turmoil in our lives. Inner peace sounded attractive. A friend was kind of enough to get us tickets to the sold-out event. That morning we packed our blanket, lawn chairs, and some snacks and headed downtown, arriving early enough, we thought, to enjoy a picnic lunch before hearing the revered religious leader speak.

As we exited the "el" train, the mobs of people obviously headed to the event in Chicago's Millennium Park added to my excitement. But when we saw the monstrous lines snaking down Michigan Avenue, my heart sank. Apparently the organizers were requiring each person to go through a metal detector and were searching every bag. Undeterred, we found the end of the line and began our wait.

After about fifteen minutes, we had moved a total of twenty feet. My husband went to see if there was a shorter line elsewhere. No luck. Another fifteen minutes, and now we were only about ten feet further along. By this time the lawn chairs were getting heavy and I was getting hungry. I started to complain about how poorly managed the event was—then felt guilty since that wasn't a very go-with-the-flow Buddhist attitude. As my husband chatted with the colorfully dressed Tibetan immigrants behind us, I did the math: We had already been in line almost an hour, and at the rate we were moving, it would be another couple hours before we entered the park.

We finally decided to give up. As we walked away from the line, I saw an Asian man taking a photo of his infant son, and I burst into tears. Overwhelmed with frustration and sadness, I ached for the little boy from Vietnam we had been waiting to adopt for over a year. My ever-supportive husband gave me a big hug and suggested we just enjoy our picnic lunch. I agreed. Why not make the best of a bad situation? We were getting good at that.

Acceptance. Surrender. Moving on.

So we found a shady spot under a big tree just outside the amphitheater area, opened our lawn chairs, enjoyed our chips and salsa, and listened to the musicians opening for the Dalai Lama. After an hour or so, I got up to find a restroom and discovered that the line had gone down to almost nothing. Deciding to try again, we packed up our stuff, made it through the security checkpoint, and found one of the last grassy spots on the lawn inside the theater. As we got situated, the Dalai Lama took the stage and sat cross-legged on his cushioned chair.

"I believe life is meant for happiness," he told the crowd of thousands, including many children—who of course caught my eye. The problem, he explained, is that people think happiness is the result of external circumstances. "Too much impatience!" he scolded light-heartedly. To find inner peace, he said, you must train your mind to have compassion for others, control your anger, and thus overcome your own suffering—whether that suffering is years in a Chinese prison, as has been the case for many Tibetan Buddhists, or the frustration and pain involved with waiting for years to have a family, as was Edmund's and mine.

❧

"This is the hardest part," my friend Mary said, barely audible over the cacophony of children at a St. Patrick's Day party where the kids clearly outnumbered the adults. My husband and I were among the few childless people downing corned beef and cabbage. Mary's daughters had been adopted from Mexico years ago, and while their wait was not excruciatingly long, she remembered how difficult it was and could commiserate. Nothing could compare to the pain of waiting to adopt, she said, not even the labor and delivery of her biological son.

Earlier that day, at an all-day adoption conference sponsored by Chicago Area Families For Adoption (CAFFA)—one of many pre-parenting educational seminars that prospective adoptive parents are required or voluntarily choose to attend—we heard it over and over from speakers, exhibitors, and fellow attendees: "The wait is the hardest part. Hang in there."

At least they get it. Those who have not adopted themselves tend to compare the wait for an adopted child to pregnancy, the way of forming families that is most familiar to them. Jokes like, "This is the longest pregnancy ever!" may be clever, but they fail to understand how an adoption wait differs from the more common way of bringing a child into a family (that, and they get old pretty quickly). News of a wanted pregnancy is nearly always a joyous event, and while the parents may be cautious during the first trimester, the next nine months are usually a time of happy anticipation. Except for those women who have experienced miscarriages or other pregnancy loss, there is rarely concern that there will not *be* a birth. And unless the child is born severely premature, the parents can expect the child to arrive within a few days, give or take, of its due date.

Not so with adoption.

Although adoption is also a joyous event, the excitement is almost always tempered by anxiety until your child is physically in your arms and legally yours. The decision to adopt often comes, as it did in Edmund's and my case, after months or years of infertility problems, miscarriage or other pregnancy difficulties. Even those who choose adoption after having biological children are somewhat nervous about how it will differ from their experience with birth children.

Once you decide to adopt, the process resembles applying for a mortgage (times ten) more than preparing for a child. The "paperchase," as it is commonly called in adoption circles, can be invasive, time-consuming, and expensive. It is not the same thing as shopping for baby furniture or other things pregnant families do to prepare for a child. Researching types of adoption, choosing between domestic or international, and finding an ethical agency is not only confusing and scary, it can become a part-time job. And another part-time job may be necessary to finance it!

After the paperwork phase has ended, prospective adoptive parents wait. Although there are estimates about how long an average family waits for a child, they are just that: estimates. No adoption is the same, and as adopting parents hear over and over again, there are no guarantees in adoption. Just because your neighbor's friend's cousin knew a lawyer who found them a birthmother in two weeks doesn't mean it will happen to you. And just because some major celebrity can sweep into a country that doesn't even allow international adoption and leave with a child the next day doesn't mean it works that way for us regular people. With wait times increasing for international adoption, the fastest growing type of adoption in the United States, a fair estimate would be that the average adoption takes anywhere from one to three years—some more, and some less.

ᐢ ᓚ

My husband, Edmund, and I met and married later in life, but one thing we knew for sure: We wanted kids. In fact, while we were engaged, I started charting my temperature every morning to see if I was ovulating so I'd have plenty to report to the doctor, whom we first visited only a few months after our honeymoon. At forty, I knew that my chances of conceiving were slim, and our doctor didn't waste any time helping us find answers. Within a year, we knew that having a biological child just wasn't going to happen for us, and we started talking about adoption.

We chose to adopt internationally because we felt a calling to be an international family. Both of us had traveled extensively around the world, and my husband had lived abroad. Our next decision involved picking a country. After research that included dozens of phone calls to agencies and, I might add, a *very* organized spreadsheet, we decided on China. My husband was attracted to Asia because he had lived there, and, to be honest, both of us were reassured by the fact that China's program had a relatively shorter wait, was relatively less expensive, and was generally considered to be the smoothest country from which to adopt.

I approached the paperwork as if it were an urgently deadlined work project and completed our home study and dossier in just over two months. Our paperwork went to China and we were logged in by the Chinese governmental office that handles adoptions. They told us that we would receive our referral (information about the child who had been matched to us) in about six to eight months. It was February of 2006, and I confidently told everyone who would listen that we would be traveling to China that fall and bringing our daughter home by Christmas. We decided to name her Sophia.

In the spring I started hearing rumblings that the wait time was increasing. Our agency sends monthly newsletters to waiting families, and they were honest that the six-to-eight-month estimate was stretching to nine to twelve. I read similar concerns, analysis, and discussions on the many adoption-related Internet listservs and chat groups I had joined and read religiously. By early summer, while many were holding onto hope that the slowdown was temporary, our agency and some others admitted that a two-year wait could be possible.

It was around this time that our efforts to adopt ceased to be something to be excited about and instead became a burden we carried with us every day. It didn't help that friends and family were getting pregnant left and right. If we got a pregnancy announcement and bad news from our agency in the same week, I would break down sobbing. As a birthmother who had placed a child for adoption when I was a teenager, it felt like some twisted poetic justice that I was facing so many hurdles now as I tried to adopt a child myself. Edmund and I started avoiding social situations because we couldn't face answering the well-intentioned questions about how the adoption was going. Looking back, I clearly was depressed.

But my natural inclination when faced with a problem is to find a solution, and by mid-summer I had come up with one: If we still had more than a year of wait time for our daughter from China, perhaps we could complete another adoption in the meantime. We wanted two children and had hoped to adopt them both before I was forty-five, so this new strategy could move things along a bit. Apparently I wasn't the only person with this great idea, and our agency assured us we could do it. They suggested adopting from Vietnam, and I began the research for an agency that handled that country.

At first, the news was promising. Several agencies would allow us to pursue both adoptions, as long as we appropriately spaced out the children, and most were excited to hear that we had much of the requisite paperwork already done. The estimate for bringing home our child was six months, and once again, we hoped for a Christmas with a baby, a boy we had already named Samuel. However, Vietnam is not known for the smooth operation of its adoption program. At that point it had only recently reopened after having been closed for several years (it has since closed again), and we hit more than our fair share of snags. I won't bore you with all the details, but suffice it to say that our Vietnam adoption did not take six months—and we did not have Samuel by that Christmas.

How did we cope? Not always that well. More than once, I wanted to give up, but my husband was strong for the both of us. "Sam and Sophie are out there," Edmund would say while comforting me during my latest crying jag. I literally could not have made it through the last three years without such a supportive partner. And I have had a few, select friends who have been extra helpful throughout this ordeal, remembering me on Mother's Day and learning the difference between DTC and LID (Dossier to China and Log In Date). Our families, too, have treated us gently, knowing when not to ask too many questions while still staying excited about their future grandchildren, nieces and nephews.

But ultimately what has helped me through the succession of grievings that followed each new announcement that, "No, you're not going to have a child yet," has been my faith. Believe me, some days I was so angry at God and stooped to wondering if this was punishment for some wrongdoing. But just as God has been with me through all the other small and large tragedies in my life—hardships that eventually helped me become the stronger person I am today—I trusted that God was with me through this painful part of life too. I saw God's presence in so many different ways: in my husband's strength, in the distraction of beauty in the world, and in the mere fact that I'm still here, ready to love these two children for whom we have waited so long.

As a Catholic, I have always found spiritual sustenance in Jesus' example, in our tradition of saints and mystics, and in the sacraments. The title of this collection of reflections is inspired by the Mass, when as part of the Lord's Prayer the priest prays, "Protect us from all anxiety, as we wait in joyful hope…" Anxiety, waiting, hope—these have been the hallmarks of our adoption journey, and God has been with us through it all. I know people from other Christian denominations, Judaism, and other religious traditions also find solace and hope in their faith, and I also have learned much from the practice of yoga and from exposure to Buddhist teaching. My own personal spiritual practices are eclectic, and that is reflected in my writings here.

As wait times for adoption increase, especially international but also domestic, those in the adoption community have rallied to support one another. With the Internet, there's no excuse for not finding someone else who is also struggling with an adoption wait. But, sadly, most churches, synagogues, and mosques remain oblivious to this particular struggle. If they offer anything for adoptive parents, it's a support group for those who already have adopted. And there are few, if any, resources out there that address the spiritual nature of this particular wait. So, as part of my own healing and in solidarity with those who are also struggling while waiting to adopt, I offer these words of commiseration, compassion, and ultimately hope.

HOW TO USE THIS BOOK

Whether you're just considering adoption for the first time, have been waiting months or years for your first child, or are going back for your second, third or fourth child, this book can help you through the good days, the not-so-good days, and the *really* bad days that can be part of the process of creating or completing your family through adoption.

You may want to start at the beginning and read a reflection each day, perhaps in the morning or before bed. Or if you're hitting a rough stretch, it might be more helpful to jump to the section, "When the Going Gets Tough" and read all of those reflections at once. Feel free to skip those that don't apply to you. The titles of the sections and of each reflection should help you pick and choose the advice you need at any given point in the process. You may read this book alone, with your partner or spouse, or as part of a support group for other waiting parents.

I have written from my own experience as a married woman pursuing an international adoption for the first time. However, wherever possible, I have tried to include the perspectives of others, including men, singles, families with biological or other adopted children, or those adopting domestically.

I hope these reflections help you survive your wait with intentionality, prayerfulness, and hope.

WHY
ADOPT?

Choices

*There are moments in our lives when we do not reason things out,
we just know in our heart of hearts
that this or that is the right thing to do.*

JEAN VANIER

❧

Anyone who has visited a Third World country, then returned home to a supermarket with an entire aisle of laundry detergents and fifty different kinds of toothpaste, realizes how much Western society is a culture of choice. I mean, my cable system goes up to nine hundred channels. Having so many choices can be a good thing, like when you love watching classic movies or when you need special toothpaste for sensitive teeth. But choice can also be overwhelming.

Adoption is full of choices. A pregnant woman may choose to avoid certain things that are harmful to her developing baby, but aside from choosing where and how to deliver, the rest of it is pretty much out of her hands. Adopting couples, on the other hand, often can choose the gender of their children, their racial or ethnic backgrounds, their ages. They can even choose to adopt more than one child at a time.

As someone who has always dreamed of having a daughter, it's nice to know that I will most likely have one. Still, all this choice can be unnerving. What if we make the wrong choice? Is it selfish to want a girl? Is it wrong to want our children to look like us or to be without major birth defects?

There is some concern that our American culture of choice has spilled over into adoption, with celebrities practically ordering "a toddler boy from Africa" off the menu. But I think most adopting parents feel uncomfortable with all the choice in adoption. And families adopting domestically learn how it feels to be on the other side, as they wait to be chosen by a birthmother.

I think these choices scare us because it feels like we're playing God with something so serious—who becomes our child—that it seems it should be left up to God. It has helped me to remember that, whether a birthmother chooses us or a foreign agency matches us with our child, God is still involved. Although we may have to make difficult choices, such as whether to accept a referral or not, I believe that if we prayerfully make those discernments we are not playing God…we are co-creating *with* God.

ᕮ ᕬ

Creator God, be with me as I make these life-changing decisions.
Help me to make good choices that will lead me to the child
who is meant to be a part of our family.

Adopting after Infertility

There is one advantage to having your life cut through to the bone.
It swiftly eliminates all the distractions and all the illusions.
The clarity of my sight is fierce. I see what matters and what does not.

PAULA D'ARCY

ↂ

Not all people who choose to build their family though adoption have suffered infertility, but a sizeable number have. Historically, adoption has been the option for those who cannot get pregnant, though today more and more families are choosing adoption as their first choice or after having biological children. Still, with women continuing to delay childbearing into their thirties and even forties, many will come to adoption after months or years of unsuccessful medical tests and procedures, miscarriages, or other pregnancy loss, and much sadness and disappointment.

What often happens, as it did in our case, is that we start our adoption journey having barely healed from the grief of infertility. This puts us at a disadvantage: Although adoption is a joyous way to create a family, the road to settling on adoption and the process itself are often pock-marked with tears, distress, anger, and disappointment. That can be even more overwhelming if you've just gotten over the pain, loss, and disappointment of infertility.

I had always been open to adoption, having witnessed several positive examples of adoptive families growing up and also choosing adoption for a child I had as a teenager. My husband, Edmund, however, was a little more leery, having witnessed several less-than-positive adoption experiences among his friends and family. But when we learned that our chances for a biological child were somewhere in the "one in a million" range, we were sure this didn't mean we weren't meant to be parents. Eventually we let go of the dream of a child "who looks like me" and began another dream: one of being an international family that includes another person who has had some tough breaks in life—a living metaphor of the diversity that surrounds us.

We came to this new dream though much prayer and soul-searching, and God was with us through it all. I don't believe God is responsible for our infertility; it wasn't some way to trick us into becoming adoptive parents. But I do believe God is helping us find new life after grief and death. That's what resurrection is all about.

⟡

God, we are grateful for the choice of adoption
as a way to build our family.
Give us the strength to weather
the ups and downs of this wild ride.

Called to Parenthood

The place God calls you to is the place
where your deep gladness and the world's deep hunger meet.

FREDERICK BUECHNER

❧

The occasion of my in-laws' fortieth wedding anniversary was my four-month-old niece's first visit to Philadelphia. Although I was excited to see her, I was also nervous since my sister-in-law's pregnancy had come as something of a surprise to us in the middle of our adoption wait. After the plane ride and my niece's first night in a strange bed, the poor little thing's schedule had been thrown out of whack and she was a bit cranky.

It turned out I was good at calming her; maybe I had the walk-and-bounce down just right. Twice I was able to rock her to sleep when others couldn't stop her cries, and my sister-in-law even asked *me* for mothering tips. Perhaps she did this just to make me feel better, but I sensed she was sincere, and it did make me feel good.

It's hard not to wonder sometimes if my infertility is a sign from God (or the universe) that I am not meant to be a mother. The increasing number of roadblocks to adoption only reinforces this fear.

Then I hear someone say, "You're so good with babies," and I realize God doesn't give talents to people to let them lie idle. I will be a mother one day, and I will be a better one for having waited and for having practiced with little Elena.

❧

God, thank you for my desire for and love of children.
Help me to share it with others as I wait for my own child.

Domestic versus International Adoption

Sound decisions are grounded in this soil—
the soil of who you really are and where you find yourself in life.

MARGARET SILF

◉◉

O ne of the first decisions prospective adoptive parents must make is whether to adopt domestically or internationally. So many other choices you will make stem from that first decision: your agency, your paperwork, ultimately who your child is. In previous generations, a closed domestic adoption was the only option. Today most, if not nearly all, domestic adoptions are open, in that the birthparents meet or choose the adoptive parents. In recent decades, international adoption has become increasingly popular, although the countries that participate are constantly changing.

There are pros and cons to each. With domestic, there is the option of receiving your child shortly after birth, of knowing your child's history and birthparents, of adopting a child of your same race. On the flip side, knowing the birthparents can present a number of challenges, and some fear the "beauty pageant" feeling of waiting to be selected and the anxiety of wondering if the birthparents will change their minds before the adoption is finalized.

International adoption sometimes offers a smoother, easier process, although it depends on each country, and the process can change without warning at any time. Some people are excited about the idea of being an international family, with children of a different race or ethnicity, and about travel to another part of the world to receive their children. However, in international adoption you are dealing with a foreign government, which is always tricky, and some families find the process to be overwhelming and the extensive travel disruptive to their families or careers.

In the Catholic tradition, there is a process of spiritual discernment, created by St. Ignatius of Loyola of Spain, that involves prayerfully evaluating the pros and cons in an important decision by imagining yourself living each option and paying close attention to your feelings with each. In this way, we can determine God's will for our life, or what some call our "vocation"—what we were put on this earth to do.

In the end, Edmund and I definitely felt called to be an international family and we chose to adopt from Asia. There have been days when I questioned our choice, usually when friends who had chosen domestic adoption came home with their very young babies, but as adoption professionals will tell you, at some point you just know in your heart or your gut where your children are.

↶ ↷

God, give us peace in the choices we have made throughout this process. Help us to prayerfully consider them.

Desire

*If I find in myself a desire
which no experience in this world can satisfy,
the most probable explanation is
that I was made for another world.*

C.S. LEWIS

❦

In religious and spiritual circles, desire has gotten a bad rap. For a culture addicted to the "gimmes," perhaps that's not such a bad thing. Anything that tries to temper the rampant consumerism and self-centeredness of our modern society should be applauded. So sometimes when I hear myself say "I want my baby now!" I feel guilty for how it makes my child sound like a commodity and me like a greedy, demanding toddler in the check-out line at Target.

But such statements also express a deep desire within my heart: the desire to become a parent, to nurture a child, to share Edmund's and my love with another helpless human being who will love us back in his or her own way. Such desire is not a bad thing; in fact, I believe it has been planted in me by my Creator. That this desire persists despite unimaginable hurdles is evidence of Someone's tenacity.

The problem is that human beings have always tried to sanctify their own desires by automatically ascribing them to God. For example, I have also had a persistent desire to live in a really nice house, but that doesn't mean that's part of the divine plan for me. A wise spiritual director once counseled me to listen to my desires and to prayerfully discern what, if anything, in them might be coming from God.

Then, this wise person said, take ownership and responsibility for your desires, and let God take it from there.

∽ ❍

God, I pray for the wisdom to discern
whether this desire for a child comes from you
and for the trust to allow you to fulfill this desire in your time.

The Paperchase

We hold the key to lasting happiness
in our own hands.
For it is not joy that makes us grateful;
it is gratitude that makes us joyful.

BROTHER DAVID STEINDL-RAST

I remember being so excited to start our adoption process. But then the enormity of the paperwork hit me when I received the list from the agency: birth certificates, fingerprints, financial documents, not to mention the incredibly long and invasive questionnaire on which I could have spent months.

If you're one of those people who's really organized—with a color-coded filing system, a personality that thrives on multitasking, and a close friend who happens to be a notary—then the paperchase may be a piece of cake. I am one of those people, but I still found it frustrating. It took up every free moment of my time for several months.

But the legwork aside, what I found difficult about the paperchase was that it seemed so emotionless and disconnected from the idea of a child. It more resembled applying for a mortgage: gathering tax returns, providing proof of insurance, writing lots of checks. It is unlike the warm, fuzzy feelings of biological pregnancy, whose tasks are all focused on the baby: going to doctor checkups, preparing for labor, decorating a nursery, and buying baby items.

I found the paperchase exhausting while I was doing it, but during our extended wait—when I had nothing to do but just sit—I longed for some task, some assignment, that made me feel like we were doing something to help bring our child home.

I got my wish: Our paperwork began to expire and much of it had to be redone!

God, help me to see all the minutia of adopting as efforts that help bring our child to us.

Attachment
and
Detachment

*The truth you believe and cling to
makes you unavailable to hear anything new.*

PEMA CHODRON

6∿9

To adoptive parents, attachment is a good thing. It's what we will try to create with our new children, even though we haven't been with them from the moment of their conception. Many of us read books or take classes on how to help children create healthy attachments. We may plan to follow guidelines for "attachment parenting"—always picking up a crying baby, not letting other people meet the child's needs for several weeks, carrying our child in a sling or carrier to help the bonding process.

It is ironic to realize that religion, especially Buddhism, teaches that attachment is a bad thing—at least for adults. Buddhists try to practice detachment, that is, an openness to whatever happens and a letting go of our expectations and desires. That, Buddhists believe, is the key to happiness not only in this life but eternally. I think Americans may be attracted to the teachings of Buddhism because we tend to get way too attached to our expectations and desires. Prosperity will do that to a country.

But other faith traditions, including Christianity, also teach detachment, in that they call on believers to trust God in all things. That's hard for control freaks like me.

Developmentally, our children need to attach. They need to have expectations that are regularly met so they learn to trust the world as a safe place in which to live and grow. But perhaps, developmentally, our task as adults and as adopting parents is to learn to detach from our desires and expectations, especially those around our adoption, in order to become better parents and better human beings.

⁘

*God, help me to let go of my expectations
during our adoption process.
I pray that I can trust you
to guide us to our child, and our child to us.*

The Home Study

I am not afraid.
I was born to do this.

St. Joan of Arc

◯◡◯

What if all parents had to write a twelve-page essay about their family of origin, life choices, and parenting skills—then explain their answers to a complete stranger—in order to become pregnant? That's what prospective adoptive parents do as part of the home study, a document compiled by a social worker who usually visits your home several times and requires a small binder full of supporting paperwork.

Although requirements vary from state to state, the home study probably causes more anxiety among prospective adoptive parents than any other part of the adoptive process. While it's true that many other people or entities may have to approve you before your adoption is completed, the home study social worker is usually the first, and definitely the most invasive.

Aside from the obvious power differential (this person has the ability to decide whether or not you get a child), there is a certain vulnerability required by adopting parents, especially for those not used to sharing intimate parts of our lives with people we don't know. (We want to appear deserving, which often leads to the most in-depth cleaning our house has received in a long time.)

Vulnerability is tricky, since it opens your heart to being hurt by the person with whom you share the truest parts of yourself. But without vulnerability, without that risk, life's deepest relationships are impossible. Our social worker, for example, was a source of so much information, advice, and even comfort, that she eventually became one of the people I believe God put in our path to help us through this.

⟋⟍

God, thank you for the people who are helping those of us who are waiting to adopt. Protect us as we make ourselves vulnerable to them.

Baby Steps

We cannot do everything,
and there is a sense of liberation in realizing that.
This enables us to do something and to do it very well.
It may be incomplete,
but it is a beginning, a step along the way,
an opportunity for God's grace to enter and do the rest.

ARCHBISHOP OSCAR ROMERO

Of course, we are all waiting for the big phone call—the day our agency calls to announce they have a child for us. But there are lots of little calls (or letters or e-mails) along the way: "You've been accepted in our program," "Your home study has been approved," "Your immigration paperwork has been completed," or "You've passed this particular milemarker required by your country."

Be sure to celebrate these steps that bring you closer to your child. Go out for a special dinner, or share the news with friends or on your website. There can be so many disappointments during the adoption process, but there are these little victories along the way too.

In the movie *What About Bob*, the self-righteous therapist (played by Richard Dreyfuss) encourages his obsessive-compulsive patient (played by Bill Murray) to take "baby steps" when he is feeling out of control in a situation. "Baby steps" became our mantra as we waited for our child.

Over time, lots of baby steps can take you pretty far down the road.

God, thank you for the baby steps that move us closer to our child.
Help us to keep our focus on the road ahead.

Anticipation

I long for You so much
I follow barefoot Your frozen tracks
That are high in the mountains
That I know are years old
I long for you so much
I have even begun to travel
Where I have never been before.

HAFIZ

❧

Some people love surprises and the feeling of anticipation that comes with them. Others peek in closets and under beds the week before Christmas. Me? I've always liked that feeling of knowing that something good is coming.

In today's check-your-e-mail-while-walking-down-the-street culture, anticipation is not exactly a popular value. We want everything on-demand: our phone calls, our photos, our music. Far too many people now take for granted our instant-gratification culture. It affects their expectations when forced to wait for the big things in life—like overcoming or recovering from an illness, or the wait for children.

My parents taught me to realize that some things, especially really good things, have to be waited for or may require some sacrifice. It's a character-building trait that has served me well. All I know is that some things are worth sacrificing for, worth waiting for, and that feeling of anticipation—the good side of waiting—is a signal that we're about to get the best present of our lives.

❧

God, I am willing to sacrifice for my child.
Bless me with the occasional excitement of anticipation while I wait.

The Cost

All shall be well. All shall be well.
All manner of things shall be well.

BLESSED JULIAN OF NORWICH

❧

It was from good friends with four biological children and four adopted children that I learned my philosophy on money: Work hard, be responsible, but then ultimately trust that God will help take care of things. My father once asked if that meant that money would fall from the sky. Sometimes it seems like it almost does.

Adopting a child is expensive. There's no getting around it. Unless you have absolutely no medical insurance and must pay for all your prenatal care and delivery out of pocket, adoption is definitely more costly than pregnancy and birth. Some adoptions cost more than others, at minimum they range in the thousands, if not tens of thousands, of dollars—in addition to all the other costs of having children. Wouldn't it be nice if the adoption agency at least gave a free car seat with every successful adoption?

Like many families, adoption has been a financial hardship for Edmund and me. We both make modest salaries and live in an expensive city. In the middle of our wait, my husband was laid off from his job and he returned to school to become a teacher. Paperwork expired and had to be redone, adding to the already steep cost of an international adoption.

But I can also say that my "work hard, be respinsible, and trust God" philosophy once again seems to be working. A family member gave us an "advance" on some inheritance money. One extremely generous friend even offered to help us with our fees. And our extended wait has actually helped financially, in that it has given us more time to save for some adoption costs that are still ahead of us. I know adoptive families who have gotten second jobs, sold off heirlooms or other possessions, borrowed money from family members, and done everything possible to help them bring their adopted children home.

Money can stir up quite a few emotions because it becomes symbolic of our issues of security, want and need, and fairness. But maybe it says "In God we trust" on our U.S. currency for a reason.

ℰ ☺

God, we trust that we will find a way to finance our adoption. Help us to be good stewards of the material riches you have given us.

Celebrity Adoptions

*Faith is taking the first step
even when you don't see the staircase.*

REV. MARTIN LUTHER KING, JR.

❧

One name is sure to incite strong feelings among nearly everyone in the adoptive community: Angelina Jolie. During our own adoption wait, the Hollywood actress seemed to grace the covers of tabloids more for her decision to adopt children than for her work in movies or even for her romantic involvements. While we were waiting for our son from Vietnam, Angelina brought home her three-year-old son from Ho Chi Minh City.

Immediately many waiting adoptive parents responded with envy: How did she get her child so quickly? It must be nice to have millions so you can grease the wheels, have your paperwork approved quickly, and spend only a few days in-country. And how dare she adopt out of the birth order? Others admired her for the work she has done to bring attention to adoption and to suffering children around the world. To them, she is a hero.

My guess is that, like the rest of us, she is somewhere in between hero and villain. In some ways, she has made my wait more difficult. If one more person asks me why Angelina Jolie brought her child home so fast while it has taken me more than a year, I will beat them with a rolled-up copy of *Us* magazine. On the other hand, seeing the face of her adorable child on the cover of that magazine and others has helped me visualize what our son might look like in a few years.

Unfortunately, our media-saturated culture tends to trivialize anything celebrities do, and an adopted child has become the new celebrity accessory. I'm not one to follow who wears what to the Oscars, and I'm getting too old and unhip to really care when someone gushes about their latest celebrity sighting. But I find myself praying for Jolie and her adopted children. Our family has become more public than I ever expected it to be—not front-page *Us* magazine famous, but public enough because our biracial family was obviously not formed by biology. And I've learned over the years, whether it is celebrities' looks, houses, talent, or adopted children, envy gets us nowhere.

ℰ ℊ

God, help me to avoid envy of those
whose children come home more quickly or easily than ours.
I pray for the success of all adoptive families—famous or not.

Referral/Match

To change the world, we must develop a spirituality for the long haul.
We must learn to do what we can in our time
knowing that God's time may very well be different from ours.

JOAN CHITTISTER, OSB

૭◡૭

There are a lot of "little" waits during the adoption process: You wait to be accepted by your agency, you wait for approval through your home study, you wait for documents to be processed, and in international adoption you wait for immigration paperwork. But the biggest wait of all, I thought, was the wait for our referral—the match with a child that comes with age, gender, other background information, and usually a photograph.

Often the wait for referral is the longest of the waits, stretching months or even years, as ours has been. During that time, I've imagined that once I know my child's face, everything will get better. It will finally feel real and we can relax, knowing that it is our turn. The only stress then will be the rush to prepare for our overseas trip and to make our home ready to receive a little one when we return—two things that I am totally willing to endure.

In my longing to get to the next step, I've forgotten how hard it must be to know that our child is lying alone in an orphanage until we are able to get there. Yes, even after the big wait, there is yet another.

Some parents who adopt domestically also know this: After waiting to be selected by a birthmother, they may have to wait for the birth of the child—sometimes a few weeks but possibly several months. For here is the frightening truth about adoption: Our child is not really our child until our little one is home with us and all the t's are crossed and i's are dotted.

But here is the good news: This waiting will prepare us for the other waitings all parents endure—waiting for our children to fall asleep, waiting for teeth to come in, waiting for them to come home from their first day of school, waiting to hear from the doctor, waiting for that college acceptance letter.

I firmly believe that if Edmund and I have learned to wait well during our adoption process, we will be better "waiters" throughout our children's lives.

e o

God, give me the strength and the courage
to tolerate and accept all the waits in my and my child's life.

**SEASONS
OF WAITING**

Spring

Out of the mud, the lotus blooms.

Buddhist saying

⟨∿⟩

It all starts with a desire for new life. Having been loved ourselves and having loved each other, Edmund and I want to share that love with someone else—a child. We are first-time parents-to-be, but others have biological children and want to expand their family through adoption, while still others have adopted before, maybe even numerous times, and are crazy enough to do it again. Somehow all of us have all decided that there is a child out there somewhere who is meant to be a part of our family.

Making the decision to adopt is not always easy. A number of us have suffered years of infertility testing and treatments with the goal of biological children. Some couples have disagreed strenuously about whether adoption is how they want to create their family before coming to consensus. But once a family makes the decision—"Yes, we want to adopt a child"—they feel the excitement of a new season, like stepping outside and seeing that the crocuses have begun pushing their way through the dirt. Bright blooms must be just around the corner.

But sometimes those flowers grow more slowly than we would like. Yes, spring is a season of tulips and green grass, warmer temperatures, and the promise of summer, but it is also a season of rain, mud, and even a thundershower or two. In Christian images, it's about Easter but it's also about Good Friday. So is the adoption process.

Like any Chicagoan who has suffered through the Windy City's winter, I am excited to see green buds on the trees and to pack away the mittens and scarves. But I also know well enough to have my raincoat and umbrella handy. In order to get to the new life of summer, we may have to wade through a few mud puddles.

❧

God, thank you for the promise of new life in our adoption,
which I realize may come
only after plenty of messiness and muddiness.

Good Friday

*Ordinary vision would stand at the foot of the cross
and say, "This is the end."
Only the eyes of faith could take in that scene
and say, "This is the beginning."*

KENNETH CHAFIN

⌒〜〇

Every year, in preparation for Easter, the holiest day for Christians, the church marks the forty days before it with Lent. It's interesting that we don't just jump into big holidays. We always have to have a period of preparation, a long runway to major holy days.

Many people who grew up in the Catholic tradition remember Lent as a time to give up candy or soda for forty days. But it is so much more. I think of it as several weeks to focus more intently on my spiritual life, a time to be a better Christian through prayer, discipline, and charity. Waiting for our child has been one of the most difficult Lenten disciplines of my life. But at least during Lent, I feel surrounded by others who are also focusing on suffering and its redemptive power. We realize that death does not have the last word; new life always comes out of it.

The pinnacle of Lenten suffering is Good Friday, when Christians commemorate the death of Jesus. I always hated Good Friday because, although we were off school, my parents wouldn't let us watch TV or play. Later as an adult, I found the Good Friday service a bit of a downer.

Then I started attending a Good Friday "Walk for Justice" that connected Jesus' suffering and death with the suffering of people around our world: innocent victims of war, starving children in Sudan, immigrants unfairly deported, mothers of children killed by gang violence. I began to realize that we all have Good Fridays in our lives—not just Jesus. In the grand scheme of things, our "Good Friday" of this adoption wait has not been as difficult as that of many people in this world.

Those whose adoption journey has been particularly difficult—with lengthening timetables, birthmothers who change their minds, or agencies that haven't always been completely honest—might consider it a Good Friday experience.

The Good News is that Easter always comes—even if looks different than what we expected.

ᴄ ⊚

God, you understand my suffering.
Be with me in my pain.
May your compassion inspire me
to be more compassionate with others who are hurting.

Easter

*Hope is what sits by a window and waits for one more dawn,
despite the fact that there isn't an ounce of proof
in tonight's black, black sky that it can possibly come.*

JOAN CHITTISTER, OSB

❧

According to the retail industry, Christmas is the biggest holiday of the year, with Halloween pretty far behind in second place. But the parish I grew up in had it right: For Christians, the most important holiday of the year is Easter—the celebration of Jesus' Resurrection, of God's ability to bring new life out of death. That parish's mission statement began with the words, "We are an Easter people."

Adoptive parents must be Easter people. We must be filled with hope for new life. We must trust that good can come out of bad. We must believe that no matter what happens—our paperwork gets lost, the country we're adopting from changes its rules, the birthmother who selected us changes her mind—God's life will ultimately triumph over these symbolic "deaths."

Of course, being Easter people doesn't mean that we wake up every day with an inexhaustible supply of optimism. Even Jesus had his doubts while praying in the garden. But our basic stance must be one of trust that this adoption will happen. Otherwise we would not have invested what we already have, both financially and emotionally.

We are Easter people. We believe.

❧

God, give me the hope of Easter to believe in new life.

Mother's Day

Before you were conceived, I wanted you.
Before you were born, I loved you.
Before you were here an hour, I would die for you.
This is the miracle of life.

MAUREEN HAWKINS

ᕫᕬᕬ

The week before Mother's Day, a member of our agency's waiting parents e-group posted a request for ideas about how to deal with Mother's Day. No one responded. It seems the pain, especially for waiting first-time moms, was too great even to discuss, and no one had any idea how to lessen it. Mother's Day is always hard for those who are not mothers but wish to be: single women, infertile couples, those who have miscarried recently, and, yes, adopting mothers stuck in the process.

As a birthmother for a closed adoption, I have often felt left out on Mother's Day. Once, shortly after I placed my son for adoption, I was in church on Mother's Day with a family who knew me while I had been pregnant. The priest asked all the mothers to stand for a blessing. The family's nine-year-old son nudged me to stand. "You're a mother, too," he said. He got it, God bless him. Today most adoptive families remember their children's biological mothers on Mother's Day, and I'd like to believe my son and his family do too.

It is a wonderful idea to single out one day a year to acknowledge and honor women who are mothers (and one way to have a good Mother's Day is to spend it with your own mother, if she is still living). But I don't think it takes away from the celebration if we acknowledge the many different ways that women "mother." There is a reason Hallmark makes Mother's Day cards specifically aimed at "Someone who is like a mother to me."

I think God has given all of us—women and men—the desire to parent, to create and to care for other living things. Let us adopting mothers celebrate that, rather than focus on the specific type of motherhood we don't yet have.

⟋ ⟋

God, help me to see and appreciate
all the ways I am a mother in the world,
while I wait for the opportunity to mother our adopted child.

Summer

It is only when you start a garden…
that you realize something important happens every day.

GEOFFREY B. CHARLESWORTH

෨✑

I'm not a gardener (in the city I can only grow herbs in pots), but my mother is. It seems as if every time I talk to her during the summer, she's just come in from the garden: planting, watering, weeding, pruning, and finally picking. And when I visit during those months, I invariably go home with a bag full of fresh lettuce, green beans, tomatoes, and maybe even strawberries or raspberries. Although I don't have to sow the seed to reap the harvest, I realize that gardening is hard work.

So is adopting a child. After the spring-like feeling of deciding to adopt comes the hard work of paperchasing—all the required forms, meetings, and paperwork to complete the adoption process. Like gardeners trying to coax new shoots into life, we get our hands dirty during this phase, and by the time it's over our backs ache.

Initially, the paperwork seemed unbearable and unfair to me. Biological parents don't have to go through all this scrutiny and work. For many of them, children seem to come so easily. For months, I felt like I had a second job. As with many couples, the work fell mostly on me as the wife, which caused some resentment. But looking back, it felt good to be doing something to help bring our child home.

Gardeners know that new life does not just spring forth from the ground without tilling, fertilizing, and tender loving care of newly planted seeds. Think of your paperchase as planting the seeds for your family, seeds that have to die in order for them to become new life. No one ever promised it would be easy. Nothing that is so worthwhile ever is.

ℰ ☉

God, be with me during the work that helps bring our child to us. Give me the strength to till the soil for the seeds of new life.

Father's Day

The most important thing
a father can do for his children
is to love their mother.

FR. THEODORE M. HESBURGH, CSC

❧

I n the second year of our wait, we were in Philadelphia to visit my husband's family for Father's Day. When we were alone in the car, I asked my husband if Father's Day was hard for him. He launched into a litany of why it was: His father had suffered from cancer, and the treatment and medications had left him in pain and unable to focus. Edmund's father is his hero, and he is terrified of losing him.

Of course, I had meant, "Is Father's Day hard for you, because you are not yet a father but have been trying to become one for three years?" Given the selflessness of the man I married, I'm not surprised he took the question in a totally different way. This other-focused attitude is just part of who my husband is. He is no navel-gazer, that's for sure.

Suffering, pain, and frustration tend to encourage us to focus on ourselves—which in turn only compounds our own suffering, pain, and frustration. Parenting (and marriage, for that matter) requires us to put our own needs behind those of others. My husband is lucky to have in his father a wonderful model of selflessness. It will serve him well when our children arrive.

❧

God, thank you for the gift of our fathers and for fathers-to-be.
Help us to shift our focus from ourselves to those we love.

Autumn

Autumn stands as an epiphany
to the truth that all things are passing
and even in the passing there is beauty.

JOYCE RUPP AND MACRINA WIEDERKEHR

❦

Remember when it was all the rage to have your "colors" done? Some beauty professional laid swatches of fabric on you and decided what season complemented your complexion. I was either a "summer" or a "winter;" I don't recall. But if there were a similar way to have your "spiritual seasons" done, I would definitely be an autumn. Fall is hands down my favorite season, and the one I missed most when I lived in the year-round summer of southern California.

I love football and cool days and wearing a wool sweater for the first time of the season. I love caramel apples and Thanksgiving and corduroy. And I love the leaves: the gorgeous colors, the sound of walking through piles of dead ones, and ironing them between wax paper. In fact, Edmund and I chose leaf-themed invitations, favors, and decorations for our fall wedding.

But fallen leaves aren't really a celebratory symbol; in fact, they're evidence of the necessary death that precedes new life—both in nature and in our lives. Autumn is the time to gather in the harvest, the sustenance we will need to make it through the long winter. It's about grieving and letting go. For me, it is the ultimate symbol of the life-death-new life process that is essential to the Christian story and so obvious in nature.

Maybe it is not surprising that I am drawn to the season of autumn, since I have have done a fair amount of grieving in my life. It's also probably true that learning to let go is the spiritual task

I have been given to learn throughout my life. During our adoption process I have once again been faced with the need to grieve and to let go and trust God. But at least I trust that spring and summer will come again. They always do.

ᕙ ᕚ

God, thank you for the seasons,
which teach that new life always follows death.
Help us to remember that
as we wait for the new lives of our children.

Holidays

Nothing happens by chance,
but by the far-sighted wisdom of God.

BLESSED JULIAN OF NORWICH

❧

For some reason, my brain works in holiday-themed batches of time. So when we completed our paperwork for our daughter in February and our agency said we would travel to get her in eight to ten months, I immediately thought, "Perfect, we'll have her home by Christmas." By the time Christmas came, the estimates had stretched out to more than a year.

So that Easter, as I was smiling at all the little girls in their frilly Easter dresses at church, I whispered to my mother, "At least we know we'll have her by next Easter." Wrong again. Not only was that too optimistic, but our son from Vietnam, whom our first agency estimated would be here "by Christmas," wasn't here by the following Easter either.

You'd think I would learn to stop hoping based on holidays. But it's hard not to. Maybe it's even human nature—or at least my nature. Holidays are special times that invariably focus on family, and especially on children. So of course I yearn to have another stocking to hang with the others, another Halloween costume to make, another Easter basket to fill.

There's no getting around it: When you're grieving—and Edmund and I are grieving our children who aren't with us yet—the holidays are going to be harder than, say, the second Tuesday of July. My own sadness has made me more aware and compassionate toward other people who also find holidays difficult: the widow or widower, the single mother, parents who have lost a child, people suffering from life-threatening illnesses.

After all, adopting parents are not the only ones who suffer and grieve.

❧

God, help me to get through the special days
that are difficult during our wait.
Teach me to be compassionate toward others
who also struggle during these times.

Winter

In the depth of winter,
I discovered within myself an invincible summer.

Albert Camus

❧

Midwesterners are hardy people. At no time is that more evident than in February. After surviving the first two or three months of winter, we get hit with the worst of it: subzero temperatures and wind chills, snow that's measured in feet rather than inches, and slippery ice on the sidewalks and our driveways.

What has always amazed and impressed my husband—who grew up in a more temperate East Coast climate—is that Midwesterners just plow right through it, both literally and figuratively. We shovel the show, put hand warmers in our mittens, and take up cross-country skiing so we don't have to spend the entire season indoors. Even at the trendier bars in Chicago, women who just paid a hundred dollars for a haircut smash it down with a good wool hat and venture out to hail a cab. I'm telling you, we're survivors.

But that doesn't mean we don't spend much of those months complaining about how cold it is. And the group bonding that results from kvetching about how high your snowbanks are or how the fluid in our eyeballs seems to be freezing actually brings us all closer. The only way to get through it, year after year, is to find some humor in it and realize that we're not alone.

At some point on the road to adopting a child it will feel like spring should be around the corner. But then—boom!—we get hit with yet another fifteen inches of snow in late March. A domestic adoption falls through; an international wait doubles or triples; a country closes its program.

Adoption is not for the thin-skinned. You need the hardy perseverance of a Nebraska farmer. An Alaskan fisherman isn't a bad model either. But know that if you just put on another layer of long underwear and make it over to the neighbor's for a cup of coffee, you will survive. We all will, together.

∽ ☉

God, be with us in the winter depths of our waiting.
Help us find a community
with whom we can get through
this seemingly interminable wait for my child.

Advent

*In this strange season when we are suspended
between realization and expectation,
may we be found honest about darkness,
more perceptive of the light.*

JACK BOOZER

❦

If ever there were a time of year that should speak to people waiting for a child, it's Advent, the four-week church season that precedes Christmas. While children are counting the days until they can open their presents and parents are counting the hours they have to finish their to-do lists, the church is anticipating an event that people waited thousands of years for: the birth of the savior.

I used to think it would be so cool to be pregnant during Advent. Not only could I identify with the pregnant Mary, I could also bask in the mood of expectant hope that pervades the church and the whole culture. Later I learned that Advent and Christmas are some of the hardest times of the year for those trying and failing to get pregnant.

It's also a hard time to be waiting for your adopted child. But at least I find comfort in identifying with the ancient Israelites who waited for the messiah. These were not people who had to wait four weeks to open their presents or even nine months for the birth of a child. No, these are people who waited their whole lifetimes, most of them dying without seeing the fulfillment of this dream.

What's important is that they waited collectively, as a people. It's the only way they could have sustained hope for so many centuries. We all need a community around us when we're waiting for something important and sacred.

Hearing all the stories during Advent about people who waited for a savior inspires me to keep my hope alive. In addition to my little community that waits with me now, I have all these spiritual forebears and models of hopeful waiting.

God, as you have throughout history,
be with me in my waiting season.

Christmas

What if God was one of us?
JOAN OSBOURNE

❧

There's no doubt about it: Christmas is for children. Presents, Santa, candy canes, shiny ornaments, and even baby Jesus—everything about Christmas seems designed to entice and entertain little kids. And the wonder and joy in their little faces on Christmas morning reaffirms the joyful hope that the birth of Jesus brings to Christians everywhere.

This emphasis on the young can also make Christmas a very difficult time for those of us who are waiting for our children. While it may help us to spend Christmas with someone else's children to try to absorb their enthusiasm by osmosis, it still leaves an empty ache for the children with whom we can't wait to spend many happy holidays.

But while Christmas is attractive to children, it is actually a very adult holiday in that it celebrates something quite serious: the Incarnation, or God becoming human and entering our physical world. This is an awesome concept when you think about it. I'm not sure if I were God I'd choose to leave the safety and comfort of my divine space and enter the messiness of life here on earth.

That our God has actually experienced human life—with all its joys as well as its pains—can be comforting to us mere mortals. Jesus had things that didn't work out as he had hoped. While Scripture does not record any stories about his adopting a child, I think it's okay to extrapolate that he understands the frustration and suffering of adopting parents.

God understands because he's "been there, done that." And that's better than all the Christmas presents you can wrap and put under a tree.

God, thank you for becoming one of us.
Help me at Christmastime and throughout the year
to remember that you understand
my human problems and foibles.

Birthdays

To everything there is a season,
and a time for every matter under heaven.

ECCLESIASTES 3:1

⟋⟍

For most of my childhood, whenever I asked my mother how old she was, she would respond, "Twenty-nine." This was her joking way of pretending she was not getting older. In her generation, women were embarrassed to admit they were thirty. Now many women enthusiastically embrace their forties and even their fifties and beyond. Still, many of us have a hard time with some of the bigger birthdays. In our youth-obsessed culture, it's still preferable to be young. Life is short, and sometimes it seems to be rushing by more quickly than it should.

During the adoption process, anything that marks the passage of time is difficult. That means holidays, seasons, and, yes, even birthdays, are no longer reasons for celebration, but rather painful reminders that twelve more months have passed without bringing a baby home. For those of us who have delayed our first child until later in life, each birthday means a later and later start to parenthood.

It's important to be gentle with ourselves during these times. My husband can pretty much predict a good cry a day or two before my birthday. Each birthday during our wait, Edmund and I have planned something special, often a small trip out of town to enjoy nature and get away from the day-to-day details of life and reminders of our wait.

I try to remember that the countries of origin of my children actually respect age more than youth. They would see another year passing as more opportunity for me to grow in wisdom before becoming a parent.

ᴄ ᴏ

God, help me to see aging
as growing in the wisdom needed for parenting.

NOT ALONE:
THOSE WHO WAIT
WITH US

Spouses and Partners

There is a faith in loving fiercely
the one who is rightfully yours.

DAVID WHYTE

೧❧

P arents often say they would rather experience their children's suffering themselves than watch their son or daughter suffer. The same is true, I think, of spouses. My husband may not break into regular crying jags like I do, but that doesn't mean that this wait isn't breaking his heart too. Every once in awhile I catch Edmund staring longingly at a dad with a baby, and I feel the depth of his sadness so profoundly that I want to just hold him and make the pain go away.

I can't erase the pain, but at least I can go through it with him. I know what he's going through and can commiserate and encourage him when he's down. And on those days when I'm tempted to call the agency and say "I give up. Cross us off the list," Edmund is strong for the both of us. Then I can hang in there for a few more days or weeks or months.

If our spouses were initially reluctant about adoption, we may be nervous about sharing our fears when the process stretches on. Though adoption definitely puts stress on a marriage, it's important for us to remember that we are in this together and that we can lean on each other for support. I often wonder if I really would have the strength and fortitude to make it through this on my own. I pray that all single parents waiting for their children have someone in their life to help them through the hard times of the adoption process.

That person will also be the one who truly shares our joy when the call comes.

༄

God, thank you for my spouse or partner.
Help me to be a source of support for him or her.

Friends Who Get It

Sometimes our light goes out,
but it is blown again into flame
by an encounter with another human being.
Each of us owes the deepest thanks
to those who have rekindled the light.

ALBERT SCHWEITZER

I have a friend from college who lives far away in Alabama now. We've only seen each other three times since we graduated almost twenty years ago, though we talk on the phone every year or two. She has had a very difficult life: a father who died while she was young, a sister tragically killed in a motorcycle accident, and finally a mother she nursed through the slow death of cancer. But she has three wonderful children and an amazing husband. She is a survivor.

Tamryn and I have spoken a few times during my adoption wait, and one time she offered this comparison: The wait for adoption is in some ways like the "preemptive grieving" people do when a loved one is dying a slow death (as compared to the grieving they do when someone dies suddenly). Later she wrote me a long e-mail expanding on this theory, including about a dozen ways that she—as a woman who has never adopted—thinks the wait must be so hard for me.

"What size baby clothes do you buy? When to have the shower? What to tell people? Some in society have yet to accept this as real parenting, so there are no rituals that everyone is on board with," she wrote. "I think this preemptive grief is probably even harder, in some ways, than watching a loved one die slowly."

Tamryn thought this was going to depress me, but I was moved to tears not by the reality she was describing but rather by the fact that this three-time biological mom understood my pain better than any non-adoptive parent I have met. She wasn't just compassionate, she actually got why I needed compassion.

Not only am I grateful for Tamryn's friendship, but I can see how the difficulties in her life have made her a compassionate person. Perhaps these challenges will do the same for me.

ꙮ

God, thank you for friends who get it.
I pray that the challenges I face during our adoption wait
help make me a more compassionate person
to others who are hurting.

Friends Who Don't

If the body is in pain, one of the first things to look for is infection.
If the soul is in pain, we might look for lack of friends.

THOMAS MORE

❦

I have more examples of uncaring friends and insensitive comments from our year of infertility treatment than I do from the later part of our adoption wait. By then I had walked or eased myself away from those who made things worse by their comments or actions, and I had trained the rest of my friends to know what I needed during this hard time.

Everyone is allowed an unintentional gaffe, not realizing that sharing how "my cousin's friend has a lawyer who got them a baby in just two weeks!" could be excruciatingly painful to hear, or not knowing that constantly being asked to defend why we chose a particular country for adoption becomes especially difficult when we are wondering why we chose the cursed country ourselves.

As hurtful as these kinds of comments can be, especially if you're already having a bad day, they only come out of the person's ignorance about adoption, and that's somewhat understandable. Our society does not yet recognize the reality of grieving that infertile and other waiting adoptive parents are going through.

Some comments came not out of ignorance but out of, well, at best, insensitivity. Many of the worst statements came when people told me they were pregnant. Any friend with an ounce of compassion had at least an inkling that it might be difficult for us to hear and they tried to express that sentiment when sharing their own joy. But there were some who were so wrapped up in their own joy that they didn't think about how their news might sound to someone like me who has waited years to have a child. I found these incidents the hardest to forgive and forget. We need to know that we have the right to distance ourselves from people who have hurt us deeply, even if they did so unintentionally. Thankfully, most friends and family were good to us through this journey.

Someday Edmund and I will be good friends to others going through this.

℮ ◎

God, we seek your comfort when friends disappoint us.
We pray to be compassionate and understanding,
and for the wisdom to know when we need to take a break.

Extended Family

A child's life is like a piece of paper
on which every person leaves a mark.

CHINESE PROVERB

⟨◦⟩

I have heard horror stories about extended family members who are completely unsupportive during the adoption wait, sometimes even opposed to adoption completely. Thankfully most parents, siblings, and in-laws desire their loved ones' happiness and do their best to be supportive. But, because they do care about us, they also struggle when they see us hurting and don't shy away from asking questions that spring from their own curiosity.

There's nothing like becoming a parent to bring up issues from one's own family of origin. Maybe that's why insensitive comments from parents, siblings, or other family members seem to hurt the most. They are the people who really know how to push our buttons.

Perhaps now, as we wait for our adopted children, is the time to start trying to establish or promote healthy adult relationships and good boundaries with our families of origin, if we haven't done that already. Soon there will be another member of this family. We owe it to our adopted children to help prepare the most welcoming new family possible.

This may mean correcting a distorted view of adoption or of our child's country of origin or educating family members about positive and negative adoption language. Or it may mean having the difficult conversation of asking some family members to avoid racially insensitive comments and jokes if we are adopting children of another race, ethnicity, or culture.

I'm not suggesting that this is easy or sometimes even possible.

But just as we lovingly prepare our child's room, we may also have to do some work to prepare the extended family that they will soon join.

℮ ☉

God, give me the courage to respond lovingly
with family members who are not supportive
or who need educating about adoption.
Help me prepare, as much as I can,
a healthy extended family for our child.

Your Child's Siblings

Both abundance and lack exist simultaneously in our lives,
as parallel realities.... When we choose not to focus on what is missing
from our lives but are grateful for the abundance...
the wasteland of illusion falls away
and we experience Heaven on earth.

SARAH BAN BREATHNACH

୭ଡ଼୨

A debate broke out on one of the popular Internet blogs for families waiting to adopt from China. The topic? Who hurts more: those waiting for their first child, or those who already have a child or children and are waiting for a sibling? Obviously this is a useless argument. Comparing pain is like comparing your children, I assume. One is not better (or worse) than the other; they're just different.

The comments on the website, however, did alert me to some of the special stresses of extended waits on families that already have children, whether younger or older. While older children and teenagers may be able to understand some of the reasons why their new brother or sister is taking so long to join their families, they still share in the disappointment. For younger children, the wait can be confusing and even heartbreaking.

And if I think it's hard for Edmund and me to time our adoption to fit our career plans and to space our two children, imagine families trying to minimize the space between their biological and adopted children as much as possible, or those trying to adopt before their teenage children leave home.

Many adoptive parents have told me that the first wait is the hardest. That doesn't mean you love your second or third any less, just that your other children are a positive distraction during your subsequent waits. But it also means that you have a responsibility to take care of the children you already have, and to model patience for them.

❦

God, thank you for the blessing of the children I already have.
Help me to teach them how to wait patiently
for their new brother or sister.

Online Buddies

The more I think about it, the more I wonder
if God and neighbor are somehow one.
"Loving God, loving neighbor"—the same thing?

FRED ROGERS

〇〜〇

What did prospective adoptive parents do before the Internet? Sure, they probably got more done at work and home without all those hours spent checking websites, listservs and blogs. But they were also much more isolated.

It's an accepted psychological principle that suffering people find support and hope just from talking with and hearing the stories of people going through similar difficulties. This is the basis of Alcoholics Anonymous, Weight Watchers, and hundreds of other support groups, whether for the newly divorced, breastfeeding moms, families of cancer patients—or Cubs fans.

A few adoption agencies have begun to offer support groups for waiting families, including my home study agency in the Chicago area. But despite the growing popularity of adoption, most adopting parents still find it easier to find a critical mass of like-minded folks online. Hundreds, if not thousands, of listservs have been created, not to mention blogs and other websites. One, the so-called "Rumor Queen," which has become a clearinghouse for information about the increasing wait for adoptions from China, gets so many hits that its server has crashed.

The information and support you find on the Internet has its pros and cons. On the positive side, there's lots of information, but not all of it is true (hence the name Rumor Queen). There are many wonderful parents online, both those who have already adopted and those who are still waiting, who are willing to share information and offer a shoulder to cry on. But some of them have their own agendas, as well. And everything you post online is being read by scores of people you don't know, perhaps even your agency director or officials in the country from which you're adopting.

Still, surrounding yourself with fellow travelers as well as those who have "been there, done that" can be invaluable. Isolation is never good.

ᨆ ᨆ

God, thank you for this technology
that gives me an opportunity
to connect with others who are going through—
or have already been through—
the wait for their adopted children.
Help me to use it wisely.

Government Officials

One who forgives ends the struggle.

AFRICAN PROVERB

❧

There is very little that is physical or "earthy" about adopting—no changing body, no ultrasounds of a growing fetus. For the most part it's about filling out forms, obtaining documents, and getting those documents approved by the correct government officials. Can you imagine the uproar if pregnant women had to depend on some bureaucrat approving paperwork in order to have a successful pregnancy?

However, I must be honest and admit that, for the most part, Edmund and I have had relatively positive interactions with most of the government offices with which we have dealt. Although there was the one notary who demanded that we jump through several extra hoops that we later learned were completely unnecessary…and my husband's birth certificate that took weeks to arrive from Pennsylvania…and the woman at the post office who missed the deadline for overnight mail because she was yakking with her coworker.

Maybe it hasn't gone so well after all.

But then there was the police officer who was willing to help us with our fingerprints, even though we arrived just as the office was closing. And the orphan unit officer at our local immigration office who helped rush our paperwork when we were up against an important deadline. And the notary at my own office who has cheerfully notarized dozens and dozens of documents, many of them multiple times. And the county court official, who didn't charge me for the copy of my divorce papers.

Most of these people—the helpful ones and the not-so-helpful ones—have no idea that in the course of their regular workday they are helping me do the most important thing I'll ever do: become a parent. They are human beings just like I am, flawed individuals who sometimes screw up. For those who go the extra mile, I am so grateful. For those who screw up, I see the opportunity to practice forgiveness.

*God, thank you for those who help me
in our holy quest for a child.
Allow me the grace to forgive
those who are unhelpful or hurtful.*

Co-workers

Just to be is a blessing.
Just to live is holy.

ABRAHAM JOSHUA HESCHEL

᠁

Aside from my husband, no one knows more about the daily ins and outs, ups and downs, of our adoption journey than my former co-worker Bryan. He was often in my office as I received e-mails with the latest news from our agency, and he is such a compassionate listener that I tended to fill him in immediately. What other non-adoptive parent knows how many days of LIDs China matched last month? Or the difference between being approved by the DIA in Vietnam and being matched at the province level? Or that your USCIS fingerprints expire after fourteen months but your I-171H expire after eighteen?

Maybe I am lucky because I worked at a religious magazine for much of our waiting period, but all my immediate co-workers were supportive of me during this long, long process. They put up with my bad moods and with the uncertainty of knowing when I would be gone to pick up the baby and for parenting leave. One woman brought me flowers when she knew I was extra depressed, and the whole department gave me a bouquet when our agency finally got licensed in Vietnam.

Not everyone has such a good rapport with their place of employment. In fact, some prospective adoptive parents share their news with few people (or no one) in their office for political or emotional reasons. Still others face special challenges, like an inflexible work schedule or a boss who is less-than-thrilled about an impending parenting leave (never mind one that keeps shifting around on his year-at-a-glance calendar).

Sometimes it helps that work can be an escape from thinking about the adoption wait, a place where, for eight hours (or more), you can focus on something else and see progress on other projects. But I would say it also helps to have some friends at your workplace, people who will understand when you're beaten down by the adoption process—and who will ultimately celebrate in your joy too.

⌒ ◎

God, thank you for the distraction of work
and for my co-workers who have been supportive during this process.
I pray that workplaces everywhere will be even more open
to the flexibility necessary for adoption and parenting.

Other Adoptive Parents

Everything that happens to you is your teacher.
The secret is to learn to sit at the feet of your life and be taught.

POLLY BERRIEN BERENDS

M y good friend Karen dreamed of adopting children long before I did. When she married a man a good decade older than she is—and one who already had a grown daughter—she thought her plan for children of her own might not happen. But as her husband, Jeff, came to see how important a family was to Karen, he got on board and eventually became even more excited about adopting than his wife had been.

Karen and Jeff started their adoption process one month after we did and also found the road rocky. Hoping for two sibling toddlers, they initially felt drawn to India and later Thailand, two countries where they encountered myriad stumbling blocks. They finally felt their children were in Ethiopia and were matched with two three-year-old twins there. Eighteen months after they started, they traveled to Africa to bring home their son and daughter.

While it is great to have online relationships with other adoptive parents, nothing beats a friend down the street. When Karen and Jeff needed someone to pick them up from the airport when they returned from Ethiopia, we were honored to be the first to meet their new kids. I have already learned so much from Karen as she maneuvers through her first months as a mother. I feel blessed to have another adoptive family among my closest of friends.

God, thank you for the gift of other adoptive parents.
Help me to learn from them
and to appreciate their wisdom and experience.

Birthmothers

Without love,
suffering has no meaning.

Fr. Fran Eschweiler

ome people pray every night for the child they're waiting for. Edmund and I do that, but we also remember another very important person in prayer: our child's birthmother. In our case, she may be an unwed woman in Vietnam who tries to hide her pregnancy or goes away to have her baby to save her reputation. Or she and her husband may decide after their child is born that they cannot afford to feed and care for an additional child. Or she may be a woman in China desperately hoping for a son because of her country's one-child policy, knowing that her husband will pressure her to abandon a daughter immediately after birth.

These women, living in extreme poverty or in rigid, patriarchal cultures, are struggling with much more difficult circumstances than I. Even in the United States, where birthmothers face less ostracism for unwed motherhood, becoming pregnant with a child you know you can't keep is gut-wrenchingly painful.

As someone who placed a child for adoption when I was a teenager, I remember well the shock of learning I was pregnant, the excruciating pain of childbirth, and the grief of making the loving decision not to parent my son. And I remember putting my young life on hold while I attended to the gestation and birth of a child I was carrying for someone else.

Back then, I imagined that my son's adoptive parents were praying for me, long before they even knew I existed. I felt that those prayers helped turn that difficult situation into a life-giving one for everyone, including me. I hope that Edmund and I do the same for a woman in Vietnam and one in China.

God, I pray for our child's birthmother,
for her health during this pregnancy,
and for peace in the difficult decision she will make.
Help this experience be life-giving for her,
as well as for our child.

Birthfathers

Why fear the dark? How can we help but love it when it is the darkness that brings the stars to us? What's more: Who does not know that it is on the darkest nights that the stars acquire their greatest splendor?

Bishop Dom Helder Camara

෨෪

There's a lot of talk about birthmothers in adoption circles: their involvement in open adoptions, adult adoptees searching for them, adoptive parents worrying about how to answer their children's questions about them. It's almost as if we forget it takes two people to make a baby. Birthfathers somehow get overlooked.

It's true that some birthfathers have removed themselves from the whole process, abandoning or refusing to marry or support the women with whom they have fathered children. Recognizing that they can't raise their children alone is one reason many women—here and abroad—choose to place their children for adoption.

But in some adoptions, especially from countries where poverty is one of the main reasons children land in orphanages, a birthfather is in the picture and may grieve the loss of his child as much as the birthmother. Edmund says he tends to imagine our children's birthmother as unmarried, while I definitely picture a two-parent family. Either way, I think it is important to remember that a man out there provided half the genetic material for our child and that someday that child may yearn for some connection to him too.

Feminist theologians have pointed out that the image of God as a father doesn't always work for some people, especially those who have had abusive fathers or been abandoned by their fathers. Although each of our children will have a loving adoptive father, I wonder if this hole in their history with their biological father will affect their image of God. I hope not. I pray they will see their biological fathers as the man who helped give them life and who loved them enough to entrust them to us.

❧

God, please watch over our child's birthfather.
Inspire him to make good decisions for himself and for his child,
and give him peace in his decision.

Other People's Children

Truly I tell you,
just as you did it to one of the least of these
who are members of my family,
you did it to me.

MATTHEW 25:40

❧

I've always said the best job in the world is to be an aunt. For example, with my sister's three children, I get to go to her house and spend as much time as I want with them—and then I can go home to my quiet, peaceful and clean home. Seriously, though, there is something to be said for being involved in the lives of other people's children, especially when you don't yet have your own. Not only is it a distraction, it's good practice.

Because my faith is so important to me, and perhaps because I am a religious professional, I have been honored to be a godparent to several children. To me, this means more than just showing up on baptism day. Being a godparent means I have been singled out to be a special person in the lives of these children, to be a partner with their parents to aid in their development, spiritually and as a whole.

Edmund and I have been named godparents of two children during our adoption wait. In some ways it has been hard. The baptism parties are always attended by lots of families with small children, which makes me ache for my own child, and by well-meaning strangers who want to hear all about the ups and downs of our adoption journey.

But if I focus on the guest of honor, the little person being welcomed into a religious community, whom we have been singled out to assist in life's journey, then it's not so hard. If I really believe that all of humanity is connected, then it is just as important that

I love this child as that I love my own—maybe even more, because this child is in front of me right now.

And someday other people will do the same for my children.

*God, thank you for the children in my life right now
and for the parents who have asked me
to be a special person in their lives.
Make me worthy of that honor.*

Your Child

For this child I prayed;
and the Lord has granted me the petition
that I made to him.
Therefore I have lent him to the Lord;
as long as he lives, he is given to the Lord.

1 Samuel 1:27-28

⤬

Whenever I start falling into pity-party mode ("Oh, we have it so hard. We've had to wait so long. Why is this happening to us?"), I remember that there is someone in this adoption equation who has it much harder than we do: our child. While I like to imagine that our son and daughter are both in the most excellent of orphanages in their respective countries, it is most likely true that they have suffered much already in their young lives. They may have spent their first hours abandoned in a public place, their bellies have probably felt hunger that most American babies never do, and they may not have known the security of a parent's consistent love.

Many adoption agencies, ours included, are careful to point out that their task is to "find parents for children, not children for parents." That's their way of reminding anxious and impatient prospective adoptive parents—many of whom, like Edmund and me, have waited so long to become parents—that adoption is really not about them. It's about the children.

While adoption professionals warn that it is unhealthy for children to be viewed as orphans who have been saved by our generosity of adopting them, it is not wrong for us to be concerned about the many children in our own country and around the world who suffer from poverty, war and other violence, hunger, and disease. Most adoption agencies also perform development work in the countries in which they have adoption programs or with unwed mothers and needy children here in the United States. Supporting these and other charitable organizations is one way to help a child who someday could be someone else's adopted child.

Because Edmund and I don't know who our children are yet, it can be difficult to think of them as actual people. We have taped up two photos to our bedroom dresser mirror: one of an infant boy from Vietnam, another of a recently referred girl from China. Both are from online friends who have already traveled for their children. They are not our son and daughter, but they help us stay focused on why we are doing all this in the first place: for them.

○ ⑤

God, please watch over our children,
whether they are born or yet unborn,
nearby or halfway around the world.
Protect them from harm and keep them safe
until they are united with us.

**WHEN THE GOING
GETS TOUGH**

The Unknown "Due Date"

Hope itself is like a star—not to be seen in the sunshine of prosperity,
and only to be discovered in the night of adversity.

CHARLES HADDON SPURGEON

⌒◡⌒

Prospective adoptive parents are divided over when to shop for baby items while waiting for a child. Some say it's better to wait so you're sure about age, gender, or timing—not to mention sparing yourself the broken heart every time you pass by the empty crib or room. Others are shopaholics like me and can't help themselves.

In the beginning, when I still thought our adoption would be completed within a year, I picked out the most adorable pink and green nursery linens from Pottery Barn. Not in a rush, I waited for a sale. One day I found the same bedding from Pottery Barn on eBay and saw that the bidding was going sky-high. A few hours of detective work later, I learned they had been discontinued. Unless I wanted to pay three times the regular prices, I had to find new linens.

Then a friend offered us her used crib. I was thrilled; it was in great condition and would save us from having to purchase one. But a few months later, she asked if she could give it to another pregnant friend first, "since you won't be needing it for awhile." Her intentions were good—to help us both save money—but I felt like a second-class mother-to-be since my "due date" kept changing and moving further into the future.

So many of the practical parts of preparing for parenthood are topsy-turvy when you're adopting. Do you dare start preparing the nursery too early? Will buying a few cute outfits lift your spirits or make you depressed? When do you allow your friends and family to host the shower? Many adopting parents are afraid to get too excited, since there's no guarantee there will be a child at the end of all this. Once things do start happening—a birthmother chooses you or you receive a referral—you may have to scramble to get everything ready in time.

It's okay to be frustrated about these kinds of things. God understands. But isn't it often true that things work out in the end? Shortly after the Pottery Barn fiasco, I ended up finding the cutest crib linens in a soft sage green—perfect for our son who came first—at one-third the price.

℃ ⊙

God, as we prepare for the child who is going to join our family,
give me the wisdom to trust that all will be well.

Jealousy

You have made us for yourself,
and our heart is restless until it rests in you.

St. Augustine

୧୬

I'll admit it: The hurting, vindictive part of me has this "hierarchy of happiness" when it comes to the seemingly endless number of pregnancies that have been announced since Edmund and I started trying to have our child. Anyone who went out of their way to tell me in a sensitive way—and many close friends did—gets my best wishes. That goes double for those who have struggled to get pregnant. Lord knows, I understand all that.

But if the announcement was something along the lines of "He just looks at me and I get pregnant," I could feel the negativity churning inside me. And those who never even stop to think how difficult it might be for us to hear their "good news," well, I find myself not bothering to stop and think about them anymore either.

This is obviously not my best self.

About a year and a half into our wait, I heard that some acquaintances from church who had just started looking into adoption the last time I had seen them already had a baby. They were shocked to get the call only a few weeks after finishing their home study. I immediately compared it to our situation: Why didn't we choose domestic adoption? What were we thinking trying to create an "international" family?

In the homily that day at church, our priest spoke about how absorption with our own problems, as serious as they may be, can prevent us from being compassionate toward others. Ouch! Then on the way out of church, I saw the newly adopted, weeks-old baby in his stroller, and my heart melted.

God did not make happiness a zero-sum game. Just because someone else is happy does mean that there will be less happiness available to us. While it's normal to feel pain that manifests itself as jealousy, there's nothing like a child—any new child—to remind you that it's not all about you.

God, curb my tendencies toward jealousy
and help me to be happy for others' joys.

Timing

Patience dispels clock time and reveals a new time,
the time of salvation.

HENRI J.M. NOUWEN

❦

B ack when I was dating and looking for Mr. Right, I was involved in several relationships that ended because of "bad timing." Usually that meant I was open to commitment and he wasn't, so the phrase would make me angry. If we were really in love, how could something like a little bad timing ruin it? Alas, I learned, perhaps we weren't really in love.

Many of us spend a good amount of energy trying to get the timing right in our lives. We struggle to meet deadlines at work, we plan vacations when we hope the crowds won't be too big, we schedule meals when we think people will be hungry. And in our personal lives—because deep down we know that we have a limited number of years on this planet—we are often frantic about timing. Jobs, promotions, marriage, kids: They all must happen by a certain time in our lives, we believe, or we fear we won't get them or that we won't be able to enjoy them adequately before our time is up.

And the timing of one thing affects so many other plans in our lives. Because Edmund and I met and married later in life, we knew we had to hurry to build our family. Because my husband was in school to change careers, we hoped our adoption travel wouldn't cause him to miss an entire semester. Because we knew we needed to buy a bigger home to accommodate our new children, we needed him to be in his new career shortly after the arrival of our first child. Then there is the spacing of children, and some families even have to try to bring home their adopted child before a sick grandparent dies.

The truth is that sometimes things don't happen when we want or need them to. Sometimes, down the line, we see that the timing was better than it seemed. But sometimes it really is bad timing. The question then becomes what to do with it. Do we become angry, resentful, and bitter? Or do we accept, with grace, the good and bad in life, becoming more compassionate in the process?

God, I pray for good timing,
but I also ask for the patience
to handle the "bad timings" in life,
whenever they occur, as they inevitably will.

Anger

With my voice I cry to the Lord;
with my voice I make my supplication to the Lord.
I pour out my complaint before him;
I tell my trouble before him.

PSALM 142:1-2

∞

Many prospective adoptive parents are afraid to get angry, even when there's plenty to be angry about. We don't want to offend anyone who is trying to help us adopt, including birthmothers, agency personnel, or even international officials. So instead we hold our anger in, or unfairly direct it at the wrong person.

Sometimes I direct my anger at our agency and its Vietnam program coordinator, since she often has to be the bearer of bad news. Other times I picture some Vietnamese official whom I've decided is evil incarnate since he's keeping our precious child from us. I rarely get mad at Edmund, because he's hurting too; but occasionally I blame him for steering us toward Asia. My co-workers also sometimes bear the brunt of my frustration with this whole process.

And some days I just get really mad at God. Why is God making me go through all this hard stuff? Why is God making my poor, innocent child wait so long for us? Why can't something in my life go smoothly and easily for once?

I realize that some people find it comforting to believe that God is in charge. But when I contemplate human suffering, I come to the same conclusions as some theologians who tried to make sense of one of the greatest human sufferings on earth: the Shoa or Holocaust. They decided that God could not have been the author of such horrible evil, that ultimately God is not omnipotent (at least not in the way that most people understand it). Instead of controlling everything that happens to us, they say, God is with us in those times of darkness, as well as times of joy.

It's normal to occasionally get mad at God. The psalmists did. But ultimately, like lashing out at my poor co-workers, it's pointing your anger in the wrong direction. God is there to help us through this.

ᘓ ᘏ

God, I am so mad!
I hope you can handle it because I need to vent.
This adoption process is painful
and I am tired of things not working out.
Help me, please.

Marital Stress

It is easy to love those who are far away.
It isn't always easy to love those who are right next to us.

MOTHER TERESA

❧

Grief counselors say that the most difficult loss for a marriage to weather is the death of a child, in part because the two partners are both grieving so immensely that one can't help the other through it. When one of us loses a parent or a job, at least the other partner is able to be there for the other person in their grief.

Although our spouses may be a great source of strength and encouragement during the adoption process, the stress of so many disappointments and frustrations also takes it toll on our relationships. What happens when we both have a "bad day" at the same time?

Well, I don't know about you, but I find myself snapping at my husband for something as silly as forgetting to soak the rice for dinner. Then he gets more easily annoyed by me and lashes out. One thing all married couples eventually learn: a fight about rice isn't really about the rice. The stress involved with adoption is added to the everyday pressures of life. Sometimes it's the straw that breaks the camel's back.

All of us bring our own baggage to a marriage or relationship, baggage that is weighed down even more by stress. The adoption process is a huge stress, and often it is added to work pressures, extended family troubles, and daily frustrations. Now is a good time to practice working through those issues, perhaps with the help of a trained counselor.

Remember when you were waiting for Mr. (or Ms.) Right instead of a child? Remind yourself to be grateful that that prayer was answered.

God, thank you for the gift of my spouse or partner.
Help me to remember that we are in this together
and to be compassionate toward one another.

Impatience

*Above all, trust in the slow work of God. We are, quite
naturally, impatient in everything to reach the end
without delay. We should like to skip the intermediate
stages. We are impatient of being on the way to something unknown, something new, and yet it is the law of
all progress that it is made by passing through some stages
of instability and that it may take a very long time.*

PIERRE TEILHARD DE CHARDIN

❧

Someone once told me that if you pray for patience, God will
send you opportunities to hone that skill. No fair! When we
pray for patience, what we really want is to get rid of the circumstances that are making us impatient. We don't really desire the
patience to endure our trials; we want our trials to disappear.

That's human nature, I think. You see it in young children
who want "mine" and, of course, they want it "now." Any disrup-
tion in their desires, wants or needs results in screams and tears.
Of course, part of maturing is learning to delay gratification and
practice patience.

But growing up doesn't guarantee a perfect sense of patience.
And when we have waited patiently for something for a long time,
it's easy to find ourselves frustrated. Early Christian leaders called
patience, or fortitude, one of the four cardinal virtues, meaning
that it is so important that other virtues are built on it. Virtues are
habits, ways of being that we must practice in order to live good
lives.

"That which does not kill me makes me stronger," philosopher
Frederick Nietzche said. "You can't always get what you want," said

a more modern philosopher, Mick Jagger of the Rolling Stones. Impatience is a call to practice patience.

*God, give me the strength
to have patience during our wait
and the maturity to know
that I can't always get what I want when I want it.*

Avoiding Despair

It is in the middle of misery that so much becomes clear.
The one who says nothing good can come of this, is not yet listening.

CLARISSA PINKOLA ESTES

❧

One of my biggest fears about our extended waiting process is that I'll be mired so long in these negative emotions of sadness, frustration, and fear that they will become a permanent part of my personality. After months or even years of this, will the good news of our referral and subsequent travel to get our child bring back the old me—the cheerful, generous, giving person who can be happy for others? I keep thinking of my mother's warning not to make a weird face "because it might stick that way."

This is how bitterness and despair differ from anger and sadness. Bitter and despairing people have their faces "stuck" in anger and sadness. Anger and sadness are normal human reactions to pain and injustice; bitterness and despair are unhealthy coping mechanisms at best. In some religious traditions, bitterness and despair are even considered sinful, not only for the way they hurt others but for the dangerous effect they have on ourselves.

It's okay to be sad and angry as you wait for your child; but it's also necessary to feel happiness and joy. Find those situations in your life—whether it's your current child's sweetness, your spouse's love, a career accomplishment, a friend's concern, or even nature's awe—and practice being happy…just so that your face doesn't get stuck the other way.

❧

God, thank you for the good things in my life.
Help me to avoid bitterness and despair.

Rude Strangers

Perhaps all the dragons in our lives are princesses who are only waiting to see us act, just once, with beauty and courage.

RANIER MARIA RILKE

❦

If one more person tells me about their friend, or their cousin, or their friend's cousin, or their cousin's friend who adopted a daughter from China, I think I might have a meltdown right in front of them. Of course, I won't. I'll just smile, like it's the first time someone has responded to my news of being a waiting adoptive parent with a story of some distant relative or acquaintance they barely know who has done the same thing, apparently faster and better than I could.

I know I'm being a bit harsh here. I'm sure that these well-meaning strangers are only trying to make some point of connection with me. After all, if you're not adopting yourself, it can seem like a rather exotic way to build a family. But it is also true that no one ever responds to a couple's news of pregnancy with a story of someone else they know who once birthed a child. Instead they just congratulate the couple and wish them the best.

Sometimes I wish some strangers could just say, "Congratulations." Instead, we have often gotten all manner of foot-in-mouth comments, from "How nice that you can pick the color of your child these days" to "Why don't you just adopt a baby from here?" Some people are just nosy and rude, but since adoption is still relatively rare, there's a lot of educating—even of good people—that needs to be done. Those of you who already have an adopted child at home know the importance of dealing with those difficult comments appropriately in front of your child.

But when you're already saddened by the latest delay or bad news from your agency, you may not be in the mood to be the public face of adoption for Rude Stranger #142. I've learned in some of our adoption classes that it's all right to say, "Wow, that's a personal question. Why do you ask?" or even just to walk away without answering. If it's someone closer to you, you can also just choose another time to point out to them why that's an inappropriate comment, rather than react on the spot.

Adoption, like pregnancy, can make you feel like public property. But it will be important for our children that we draw some boundaries when it comes to sharing our family's story. It couldn't hurt to start practicing now.

God, give me the wisdom to deal patiently with people who are not sensitive to our pain during this time of waiting.

Fear

Perfect love casts out fear.

1 JOHN 4:18

❧

For much of my life, I lived out of fear. I was afraid I wasn't good enough, popular enough, or pretty enough. I was afraid that the world was a scary place, and that bad things would happen to me if I wasn't careful. I was afraid that if I didn't work really, really hard that I might end up without all the things I desired: a home, love, children.

Fear is a powerful motivator for individuals and for entire societies, but it takes a toll on the psyches of those who live constantly in it. Later in life, as part of some spiritual and psychological self-development, I learned to trust and live out of love, but that more optimistic stance still is not second nature to me.

So when the adoption process started hitting snags, it was easy for me to revert to my old ways of fearing for the worst. What if Edmund and I never get a child? What if our child has severe problems and never attaches to us? What if adoption costs so much that we end up too poor to buy a house or send our children to good schools?

I have to force myself to think more hopefully: What if our child coming later means we have time to work on our marriage in a way that prevents problems later on? What if waiting means we are matched with the perfect child for us? What if the challenges of adoption force us to meet people in similar situations who will become friends for life?

I'm not one who believes that God directs everything that happens here on earth. That's why I rarely pray for God to help bring our child to us more quickly. But I do believe that I can trust God to help me and be with me through whatever happens in life. Having that trust is scary sometimes, but in the end it feels better than constant fear.

⤳

God, I trust you.
Help me to banish fear from my mind and my heart.

Positive Thoughts

Trust in the Lord with all your heart,
and do not rely on your own insight.
In all your ways acknowledge him,
and he will make straight your paths.

PROVERBS 3:5-6

ॐ

Some people believe that we can actually control what happens to us in life, just by virtue of our positive or negative thoughts. Popularized by the book and movie *The Secret*, the philosophy is based on the theory of attraction of like energy.

I think there's some truth to it. We've all known people who always seem to be obsessing about their latest trouble, and, lo and behold, more trouble finds them. It is true that every experience has its positives and negatives, and ultimately we decide which to focus on.

On the other hand, I don't think it's helpful for people going through immense suffering to be given the added burden of feeling that they've brought it upon themselves. A *Saturday Night Live* sketch mocking *The Secret* portrayed the author sending copies of the book to starving refugees in Darfur, Sudan, and encouraging them to just think good thoughts.

While I don't believe God is responsible for all the suffering in the world, neither do I believe that I am. And for control types like me, any philosophy that says I control everything in my life can be counterproductive when I should instead be learning the spiritual lesson of letting go.

But we do have some choices in a seemingly otherwise uncontrollable situation: Will I focus on the good in my life today? Or will I obsess about the negative?

God, give me the gift of optimism today,
so I can focus on the positive things in my life.

Sadness

We must begin by accepting the fact
that we are pilgrims on this earth,
destined to be partially restless and unfulfilled,
living in a world in which all symphonies remain unfinished.

Fr. Ronald Rolheiser, OMI

ust when you think everyone you know has announced their pregnancies to you, they start announcing their second (or third or fourth). When your adoption wait stretches into years, that can happen. Obviously these are people I love, and I am truly happy for them. Deep down I know that their happiness is not causing my unhappiness; the two are not related. But their happiness sometimes has the unintended consequence of highlighting my sadness.

It's hard to be sad. Anger and frustration seem so much more constructive. At least you're getting mad and venting it. But sadness just sits there, gnawing at your guts day in and day out until you can hardly feel anything anymore. At a certain point, you're pretty much all cried out. Some days the only reminder of my sadness is seeing someone who is truly happy and realizing, "That's not me."

Without witnessing others' happiness, it's easy to forget how sad you really are. It's even tempting to surround yourself with people who are more miserable than you are to somehow make you feel better. Focusing on gratitude for the good things in my life at least helps me get out of bed in the morning.

Sure, I'd like to be blissfully happy as much as the next person, and I'm no masochist who desires pain. But I also recognize and accept that life is not fair, and that many people suffer, many of them much more so than I. My faith has helped me find meaning in suffering, while not wallowing in it. Sadness can be transformed into compassion; pain can give us perspective. God does not abandon me in my sadness.

God, I know you never promised me an easy life.
But it hurts to be sad for so long.
Help me to deal with this pain.

Joy

*Time spent laughing
is time spent with the gods.*

JAPANESE PROVERB

❧

My friend Kristen says she wakes up many mornings to the sound of her eight-month-old son just bursting with giggles. Her husband, who gets up with the baby in the morning, will start laughing and it's infectious. Eventually the two of them are in stitches with laughter that carries up to my friend's bedroom. What a wonderful alarm clock!

Scientists have found that when we laugh, certain chemicals released in the bloodstream give us a little "high." When I was going through a particularly difficult time in my life, a co-worker prescribed Woody Allen movies. It worked. Any distraction from pain can help you get through one more day, and a distraction that makes you laugh is even better.

Sometimes those of us going through the adoption process tend to become very serious. This is a life-and-death kind of matter, after all. We are talking about children's very lives and our own most precious dreams. But, as with any serious problem, sometimes it helps to lighten up.

I do believe God intends for us to be joyful, which is different than being happy. Happiness implies that everything is going swimmingly, that it couldn't be better. But joy is a state of mind that exists despite our outside circumstances. It is a trust that all will be well.

It's hard to be joyful when there's little to be happy about. Sometimes it takes a shift in focus, from our problems to those things for which we are grateful. Or sometimes it takes a Woody Allen movie.

God, give me glimpses of joy in my life and in the world. Help me to not lose my sense of humor and of wonder during these trying times.

COPING
STRATEGIES

Keeping Busy

Don't be timid.
Load the ship and set out.

RUMI

❦

I find myself drawn to the countercultural movement of Americans who are trying to step back from the busyness of twenty-first-century life. Some have moved out of cities to more rural environs; perhaps they have dropped out of the corporate rat-race in exchange for employment that is more meaningful or family-friendly.

In my twenties and thirties, I wore my exhaustion on my sleeve like a badge of honor. Any get-together with friends inevitably included the conversation in which we all tried to one-up one another with the long hours we kept at the office, the number of project deadlines on our calendar, or even the social and recreational activities eating up our days. A few years ago—around the same time Edmund and I started trying to have a family, not coincidentally—I started craving more time to chill, to just hang out with my husband, friends, and family.

But instead I am as busy as ever. My employer has cut back on staff, leaving me to do the work of one-and-a-half people; obligations to my family and friends have increased as my husband and I begin babysitting for their children and entertaining more; and several freelance projects have fallen in my lap, including this book.

I usually think of busyness as something I pray to God to deliver me from, or as something that a more spiritually devout person would shun. After all, often people hide from God—and from their true selves—in their busyness. But lately I've been thinking that God has sent some of this busyness to me on purpose, to help distract me from the wait and to encourage me to put my energy in the service of others.

❧

God, thank you for these worthwhile projects I have right now. Help me not to use them as a way to escape from you or to hide from my problems, but rather to do good work while I wait for my children.

Slowing Down

Stopping is a spiritual art. It is the refuge when we drink life in.

SUE MONK KIDD

While busyness can be helpful in distracting me from the sadness of the wait, excessive distraction can be dangerous. We don't want to forget how to feel, even if what we feel now is mostly frustration and sadness. Friends who are physicians-in-training have told me that when they learn to turn off their emotions to handle life-and-death situations, they run the risk of not remembering to turn them back on. As adopting parents, all of us want to be able to feel the joy and exhilaration when our good news comes.

I admit I sometimes have become numb during our wait. Some days I just can't handle the negative emotions, so I do everything I can to not feel anything, including avoiding my own thoughts. If this goes on too long, however, it can easily become depression.

If we don't want to forget how to feel, we need to find times for quiet reflection to get in touch with those feelings. It might be as simple as a quiet walk in the woods or park, or a yoga class, or time to journal.

Listen to your soul: How much feeling can you handle today? Just make sure the answer isn't "none" too many days in a row.

God, grant me peace in my silence.
Help me to be able to handle the sadness,
frustration and even anger I sometimes feel
while waiting for my child.

Creativity

At the back of our brains, so to speak,
there is a forgotten blaze or burst of astonishment
at our own existence.
The object of the artistic and spiritual life
is to dig for this sunrise of wonder.

G.K. CHESTERTON

❧

Would you believe it if I told you knitting saved my sanity during our adoption wait? It's true. Knitting while watching TV or movies was a distraction, and the rhythmic repetition was meditative and calming. But that's not all. I think it also satisfied, in some small way, the creative urge that is part of our desire to become parents.

I've always been a crafty person. My mother sewed and knit; her mother made beautiful lace. My other grandmother was a home economics teacher and proficient in all the domestic arts. So I learned from the women around me the satisfaction of watching things come into being. There's something about finding the perfect yarn for a project, then winding it into a ball, casting on, and beginning to knit. First you have an inch of what could be anything. Then slowly it shapes into a hat, a mitten, or a sweater. As my mom says, you just follow the pattern, line by line, and eventually you'll get to the end.

If we believe that God created us and that we are made in the image of God, then we must contain the creative urge as part of our make-up. Parenting—both biological and adoptive—is one way we respond to that desire, whether by physically creating babies or creating our families through adoption.

Much of what I've been knitting are baby sweaters. As is often the case, while we are going through the long process of adoption, nearly every one we know, it seems, has become pregnant and had a child. For a knitter, the handmade baby gift is a must, for close friends anyway. Sometimes it's hard, and I've had to put a few projects aside while I wallowed in my own grief. But how can I not celebrate the new life in these families, whether by birth or adoption? How can such adorable little children go without hand-knit sweaters?

God, you placed this creative urge deep in my heart.
Help me to respond to it in ways that serve the world.

Letting Go

Spring comes,
and the grass grows all by itself.

BUDDHIST SAYING

⟨∿⟩

For my birthday, my husband gave me a massage. Actually, *he* didn't give me the massage, but he paid for it—one by a professional massage therapist, and it was wonderful. As I lay on the heated sheets, my face held by the padded rest, the smell of lemongrass oil in the air and soft piano music in the background, she told me my only job was to relax and to not try to help her. "Just be like a wet noodle," she said.

Then she proceeded to try to work out all my tension and stress—which apparently I hold in my upper back and shoulders. With her incredibly strong thumbs, she found the knot in my mid-back and repeatedly rubbed it, using long strokes that ended down my arm. She lifted my arm ("Stop trying to help me. Remember: wet noodle.") and let it dangle off the edge of the table. I could feel all my worries and pressures leaving my body and dripping off my fingertips. I was letting them go.

I've come to believe that—for me, anyway—letting go is the most difficult spiritual lesson, and one I have to keep learning over and over. I am not in charge of everything. I need to learn to trust: myself, other people, a Higher Power.

With our adoption, I initially tried to control everything, from the paperwork to the people who worked at our agency. But slowly I came to let go, mostly because the process continually showed me that I literally had no control over whether or when we received our child. Yet I accepted that detached attitude begrudgingly. I am now working on truly embracing it, seeing it as a healthier, more faith-filled way of living. If I let God be God, then I can tend to the business of being a better human being.

The morning after my massage, I awoke with a deep soreness in my back, the kind you have after a strenuous work out. Apparently letting go is hard work.

☙ ❧

God, teach me to let go and to trust you,
even if it hurts.

Beauty

The world will be saved by beauty.

FYODOR DOSTOEVSKY

❧

While traveling in the slums and poor villages in India a few years ago, I was struck by the beautiful silk fabrics of the women's saris, their stacks of colorful bangles on their wrists, their many rings, and other jewelry. In the midst of much poverty and filth, they seemed to be railing against the ugliness. We all have a God-given need for beauty, and it can be especially healing during difficult times.

Many people find beauty in nature, in the warm colors of a sunset or the awesome stature of a sequoia tree. Others appreciate the beauty in fine art or popular art, whether a Monet painting or a song by U2. Some see beauty in an exquisitely prepared meal or well-designed building.

It is also possible to find beauty in the everyday: in the lovely fabric of a new skirt, the sparkly granite of a countertop, the soft pinks of roses in a garden. I live in a big city but I see beauty everywhere, from the carved friezes of a downtown building to the headdresses worn by Nigerian women at my church. But when I find that I am no longer appreciating the beauty of my own surroundings, then I know it's time to get out of town to freshen my eyesight.

All of this is good practice to prepare for appreciating the most beautiful thing of all: the first sight of our child.

❧

God, thank you for the beauty in the world that reminds me of you.
Give me eyes to appreciate the beauty around me.

Getting Away

We shall not cease from exploration
And the end of all our exploring
Will be to arrive where we started
And know the place for the first time.

T.S. ELIOT

❧

About six months into our adoption wait, my husband and I planned what we called "Our Last Hurrah," a ten-day trip to Paris and the south of France. This was to be our last globetrotting trip before we had kids, my chance to see a part of Europe I had never before visited. Although we weren't able to completely escape our sadness over our not-yet family, we did find it helpful to leave behind the everyday routine of our lives, explore another country a bit, and spend time together sipping wine, taking long walks, and just relaxing.

Of course, if I had known then that our wait would be as long as it was, I would have called it "One of Our Last Hurrahs." We haven't made anymore overseas trips (money being tight during the adoption process), but we do make a point of getting away to nurture our spirits while we wait. Even if it's just a night at a B&B a few hours away or a weekend at my parents' lake house when they're out of town, we have found that even a mini-vacation can steel us for the ongoing work of hanging in there while we wait for our children.

Trips to visit family, other holiday gatherings, and work travel don't count. A healing vacation not only takes you away from your everyday grind, but it must also transport you to another world, either literally or figuratively. The point is to come back spiritually renewed and ready to face our lives' challenges. This was part of the ancient spiritual practice of pilgrimage, in which people found

God while on the road in a way they couldn't have if they had just stayed home.

We still anxiously await our "big pilgrimages": our trips to China and Vietnam to bring home our children. While the anticipation for the big trips is exciting, we realize that we need more "instant gratification." So we pack our bags and head to Michigan or Wisconsin (almost foreign countries, some might argue). Each trip satisfies our wanderlust spirit and gives us the new eyes of the pilgrim returning home.

℮ ◉

God, give us the renewed spirit of a pilgrim,
whether we have traveled across the world or across town.

Breathe

Breath is the bridge which connects life to consciousness,
which unites your body to your thoughts.
Whenever your mind becomes scattered,
use your breath as the means to take hold of your mind again.

Thich Nhat Hanh

∽

Because a good friend of mine became a yoga teacher about ten years ago, I joined the yoga craze. At first, it was just a good workout. I discovered muscles I didn't even know I had, and it was cool to see my flexibility increase so that, yes, I could put my foot behind my head.

But yoga quickly became a spiritual practice for me as well, and I have learned many deep lessons "on the mat." I've learned the importance of letting go of expectations, of opening my heart, and of regular practice. But the most important thing I have learned from yoga is how to breathe.

Breathing, like most bodily functions, is something we take for granted until we have a problem with it. A bad cold with a stuffy nose can make us grateful for unimpeded airways. Many Eastern religious traditions put a strong emphasis on the importance of mindful breathing, whether during mediation or other exercises. To someone who has never done it, it's hard to believe that merely slowing down your breathing and concentrating solely on it can alter your consciousness in any way. But medical tests have proven that conscious breathing immediately affects our physiology, lowering our heart rate and other symptoms of anxiety.

I don't think it's a coincidence that the word for "Spirit" or "Holy Spirit" in the Bible can also be translated as "Breath." Christians often picture the Holy Spirit as a dove or a flame, but maybe a better image is the invisible air we breathe. And when we bring the Spirit of God deeply into our whole body, through intentional, conscious breathing, we can't help but be renewed and transformed. And that's even better than being able to put your foot behind your head.

℮ ☉

God, help me to feel your presence in every breath I take.

Living in the Present

*Happiness consists in finding out precisely what
that "one thing necessary" may be in our lives,
and in gladly relinquishing all the rest.
For then, by a divine paradox,
we find that everything else is given us,
together with the one thing we needed.*

THOMAS MERTON

❦

Whenever I would call our agency director for an update,
she would give me the news about our wait in "best case
scenario" and "worst case scenario" format. Although
my heart would leap at the possibility of the "best," I would force
my mind to accept the "worst." Preparing for the worst is one way
to keep your expectations in check, so that when bad news comes,
you're not shocked by it.

One of the hardest parts about building your family though
adoption is not being able to make definite plans for your child's
arrival. Should we take that vacation this summer? Will we be able
to attend our niece's graduation? When will I be absent from the
office for any parenting leave?

If someone would have told us when we started that it would
take almost three years to get our first child, we would have been
disappointed at the length of the wait but we could have coped
better. Instead, being told every few months that it would be "a
few more months" is like some psychological version of the toy on
a string that keeps getting tugged away from you.

Having expectations for the future is normal, perhaps even
more so in a culture that is so focused on getting to the next thing.
But one way to temper them is to turn our attention to the present,

which is a spiritual practice in Buddhism. If you are washing the dishes, Buddhism teaches, focus only on the dishes, not on what you are planning to do next. If you give your full attention and intention to the task at hand, it will become a holy act.

Take a tip from the Buddhists today: Ignore that toy on the string and focus on what needs your attention right now.

ℭ ◎

God, help me let go of expectations today.
As much as I anticipate the future with our child,
help me to live consciously in the present.

Act As If

If a man wishes to be sure of the road he treads on,
he must close his eyes and walk in the dark.

St. John of the Cross

Recovering addicts are some of the most spiritual people I know. Whatever their religious affiliation—and sometimes they have no ties to organized religion—people who follow the Twelve Steps have learned the basic spiritual tenet that God is God, and we are not. So they have to trust their "Higher Power" completely. "Let go and let God," they say, and they mean it. Twelve-Steppers are completely clear that they cannot kick their addiction without God's help.

As several friends with addictions have taught me, this is not easy, and they had to attend regular meetings, sometimes every day, to get the support necessary to live in such a radical attitude of trust. And even then they regularly screw up and have to start all over again the next day.

Another Twelve-Step tip applies to when you are losing faith that something will happen or that you will be able to make a change in your life. Then you "act as if" that change or event has already happened. "Fake it till you make it" is another way of saying it. (As you can see, Twelve-Steppers have a fondness for clever sayings to help you remember the advice when you're struggling.)

How can this apply to the adoption wait? Obviously it does not mean avoiding reality, or living like you have a child when in fact you do not. But on those days when I want to give up, when I am losing my belief that this will ever happen, I "act as if" my child is coming as surely as most third-trimester pregnancies end with a baby.

Hope is hard work. Sometimes you have to "fake it till you make it."

God, give me the strength to let go
and trust that my child will come,
as surely as the sun will rise tomorrow.

Nature

The trees and stones will teach you
what you never learn from the masters.

ST. BERNARD OF CLAIRVAUX

❦

Why is it that so many of those who claim the "spiritual but not religious" moniker say they would rather go hiking than go to church? I think this says something about the quality (or lack thereof) of some religious services, but more importantly it reveals the truth that so many people experience God in nature.

Even those of us who are religious *and* spiritual have to admit that some of our most memorable experiences of God's power have been at the foot of a waterfall or at the edge of a canyon. Celtic spritualists refer to these as "thin places" where the barrier between the mortal and the divine is more easily bridged. No matter what you believe about how creation happens, most people can't help but be awed by the beauty of majestic mountains, the ocean, or even a little grasshopper. The grand power of natural forces or the intricate beauty of a tiny animal demands a certain level of respect.

As more and more of us live in urban settings, we realize how much we need to escape into some form of nature to get grounded, to slow down enough to have time to think and pray. That may happen in a national forest, or it may happen in the corner park. For me, as long as there are trees, I feel like I've gotten back to nature.

People who build beautiful churches are trying to recreate the awe-inspiring, prayerful environment that nature first provided. I find that it's good to pray in community in churches, but sometimes I can best commune with the Divine on the beach. When I'm having a hard day and can't handle seeing all the families at church, it can be easier to find God and pray alone in nature.

༄

God, thank you for the natural world you have given us.
I am grateful for the opportunity to see you in it.

Ritual

My life is my message.

∽

My friend Karen and her husband, Jeff, were leaving in a few weeks to pick up the three-year-old twins they were adopting from Ethiopia. Our faith traditions and culture offer baptism and a bris for infants once they're born and baby showers for women who are pregnant. But our women's spirituality group needed a different ritual to bless Karen as she was launched into motherhood. So we made one up.

We met on a Saturday evening, ordered Ethiopian food for dinner, and caught up on each other's lives. Then we gathered in the living room, where an altar had been set up with a candle, flowers, photos of the children, and a few artifacts from Ethiopia. We opened with a prayer. To honor the creativity involved in all kinds of "mothering," we placed a pile of children's art supplies in the middle of the coffee table, and each women took one and explained how it reminded her of Karen's qualities as a mother. For example, the modeling clay spoke to her adaptability, the fuzzy pompoms to her nurturing personality.

Then, to bless the children, we each drew a symbol on a square of cloth to symbolize our wishes for her new son and daughter. An open door meant opportunity, a map of Africa stood for their culture and heritage, an Ethiopian cross symbolized faith. Those fabric squares were later pieced together to make a wall quilt for the children's room. Finally, we all placed our hands on Karen and prayed that God would watch over her during her travels and as she began her life as a mother.

Although the adoption process has developed its own set of rituals—the home study, the referral, the travel blog—our faith traditions have not caught up with formal rituals for adopting parents. Ritual is so important for marking the stages in our lives. If the right ritual doesn't exist, don't be afraid to create your own.

ℰ ☉

God, help us to pray together in new ways
to mark the holy times in our lives.

Gratitude

If the only prayer you say in your whole life is "thank you,"
that would suffice.

MEISTER ECKHART

There's nothing like another person's tragedy to help me remember to be grateful for what I have. During our adoption wait the world was beset with some horrendous natural and man-made disasters. Whenever I felt myself planning a pity party about our wait, all I had to do was watch the evening news.

Every morning when I wake to National Public Radio's top news stories, which invariably include someone who has died in war or as a victim of crime, I imagine the family that will receive the news that a husband or wife, son or daughter, brother or sister, will not be coming home. After the horrendous news of Hurricane Katrina, the tsunami in Indonesia, the earthquake in Pakistan, I can't help but count my blessings that I have a roof over my head and my material possessions intact, not to mention the health and safety of my loved ones.

The latest crises throughout the world remind me to thank God for the affluence we as a country and I personally experience. Although it has required penny pinching and creative financing, in the end Edmund and I are at least able to afford adoption.

More than just helping me to be grateful, these serious world tragedies force me to recognize how small, in comparison, my own difficulties are. Instead of focusing on myself, I can't help but be moved to have compassion for all those who are truly suffering.

God, I am grateful for all the blessings in my life.
May they make me more compassionate for those in need.

Service

*True compassion does not come from wanting to help out
those less fortunate than ourselves,
but from realizing our kinship with all beings.*

PEMA CHODRON

While I have been waiting for my own daughter, four other little girls came into my life. Ruiza, Farida, Albina, and Songul are part of a Turkish refugee family from Russia who came to America to escape persecution. When Edmund and I volunteered with a program that helps newly arrived refugees, we were matched with the family we call "the Uzbeks" (because they are originally from Uzbekistan).

Our task was to meet with the family once a week and help them practice their English. But our visits became so much more than that; over time we all became friends. Nasiba, the mother, would cook traditional foods for us, I took the kids shopping for school supplies, and we all shared stories about our lives.

Eventually we told them about the adoption, finding China— and later Vietnam—on a map. Of course they asked why we were not adopting from Russia and we explained our choice. After a year they moved to the suburbs to be near family, and we only see them occasionally now. But the four girls still scream my name and run to greet me when I arrive, and I find myself so in love with this family that I can hardly believe it.

It's a cliché to say that those who do service work get more out of it than they give, but it's also true. I had all this love in my heart to give to our own children, and instead of keeping it tucked away somewhere, I shared it with four little girls who needed it. Then I realized I had as much love—if not more—as when I started.

Someday we are going to visit and bring our son and daughter to show this family. I can't wait for them to meet each other.

◦ ◦

*God, help me to give my time
and my love to those who need it in our world.*

Exercise

You do not have to be good.
You do not have to walk on your knees
for a hundred miles through the desert, repenting.
You only have to let the soft animal of your body love what it loves.

MARY OLIVER

❧

A bunch of waiting parents on an Internet group have decided to use this time to get in shape and lose weight. Good for them. Me? I've actually gained a few pounds, mostly because I have coped by throwing myself into my work, which means two unhealthy habits: snacking at my desk and no time to work out.

I used to work out daily, back when I lived in a high rise and only had to take the elevator to the gym. Now I'm lucky if I get on the Stairmaster once or twice a week. I do walk a lot and still regularly do yoga, which is not only a physical but a spiritual practice for me. All exercise can be a spiritual practice if we remember that our bodies are holy temples of our spirit and of God's.

As I age, I am realizing how important it is not to take my health for granted. Little aches and pains that weren't there a few years ago are starting to show up. While our consumer culture tells me that if I buy this cream or this pill I can look young forever, I'm not fooled. We all get older, but we can stay as healthy as possible.

And we're going to need all the energy we can get when we have little ones to chase.

❧

God, thank you for the gift of my body.
Help me to keep it healthy enough to chase around two kids!

SPIRITUAL
RESOURCES

Faith

If you could understand a single grain of wheat,
you would die of wonder.

MARTIN LUTHER

⌒〜⌒

R eligious people, by definition, are supposed to be people
with faith, but after experiencing the crankiness of many of
them, you'd never know it. You would think they don't
really believe in God, given the way some of them admonish others for their choices or try to interpret God for everyone else. But
truly spiritual people live with a peacefulness and hope that's hard
to miss, and it becomes extra evident when they are facing a chal-
lenge in life.

I'm sure it was hard for my friend Lourdes as she watched one
woman after another in our group of friends marry. About seven
or eight of us had been meeting as a women's spirituality group
for years, and even though we had officially disbanded, we still
gathered socially and for important milestones, like weddings and
baby showers.

Although some days she was sad that she hadn't found Mr. Right
yet, I don't think she ever lost faith. And I know that faith came from
a deeply spiritual place, grounded in Catholicism but also nurtured
by Eastern religion and yogic teaching. So I wasn't surprised when
she finally met a wonderful man and married him.

This is what faith truly is—not merely assenting to a list of
beliefs, but truly living as if you believe them. Do we really believe
that God created this world and proclaimed it "good"? Do we really believe that God knows what it's like to be human and thus
shares in our struggles? Do we really believe that there is something
beyond this world, that life can truly come out of death? Do we

really believe that God did not give us this desire and calling to be parents only to sadistically make it impossible for us? Do we believe?

God, I believe in you
and I trust that you will walk with me
during this journey to our child.

Prayer

"Help" is a prayer that is always answered.

ANNE LAMOTT

◖◗

I was dreading a work conference that I attend twice a year. This would be the third meeting where I would be showing up, after telling my colleagues that for sure I would miss the next one because I would be traveling to get our child or would be out on parenting leave. Once again I would have to explain that, no, we haven't even been matched with our child yet.

But this is a group of religious journalists, so maybe I shouldn't have been surprised at the sensitivity with which they cautiously asked, "Any news yet?" and the sincerity with which they said, "You have been in my prayers." To which I responded, "I know. That's why I haven't given up yet."

In other words, somehow the prayers of all those people who love me have sustained me during our wait. Surely their pleas to heaven have not resulted in a quick referral (although who knows how much longer it could be without them), but knowing that so many people realize the injustice of it all and call on their God to bring us some relief—well, that alone brings relief.

There have been studies that show that patients who have people praying for them recover faster than those who don't, even if they aren't aware that they are being prayed for. I don't know how it works, but it seems to me that you can't pray for someone or something without caring about them or it. And anything that increases caring in the world can't be a bad thing.

Edmund and I pray for our own situation, of course, but most of our prayers are for the needs of others as well. Perhaps by taking us out of our own worries and concerns, prayer helps us see that our problems are not unique and in many ways not as difficult as those faced by others. We all share in the struggles of life, and we all get through those struggles with the help of others who care.

⌒

God, I know I come to you
with so many requests and needs.
Thank you for listening.

Sabbath

A life less planned is better.

BLESSED JOHN XXIII

∽

I learned how to relax from my friend Caroline. Back before she had four children, she and her husband loved to have "blob weekends" in which they did nothing more strenuous than go out to dinner and read the New York *Times*. They even came up with a name for the feeling on Sunday night when you start thinking about work again: "the dreads."

I, on the other hand, was a busybody who thought weekends were a time to accomplish everything I couldn't do during the week. But once I learned how to "blob," I realized how rejuvenating it can be and that I am more productive later for having rested.

The concept of Sabbath—a specific time for rest and for God—is practiced in several religious traditions, but perhaps most prominently in Judaism. Jews trust that nothing is so important that it needs to be worked on or worried about seven days a week.

This can be true about our adoption process as well. Sometimes we need to just "give it a rest" and take day off. Today many people in our hyper-productive, stressed-out world are trying to reclaim the practice of Sabbath by making more time with family and their faith community instead of working 24/7. It's even better than "blobbing."

∽

*God, I am grateful for the opportunity
to take a break from my worries at least once a week.
Help me cultivate the practice of Sabbath.*

Mystery

*I would rather live in a world
where my life is surrounded by mystery
than live in a world so small
that my mind could comprehend it.*

Rev. Harry Emerson Fosdick

૭❨❧

I'll be honest with you: I think that some of the people the Christian tradition has named "mystics" in past centuries were probably suffering from what we now would consider mental illness. Come on, some of those stories are really weird. But then being a mystic always sets someone apart from the rest of the world that merrily goes along with its business without attending to the deeper part of life.

Yet I have been inspired by many of the mystical teachers throughout history. Hildegard of Bingen, a twelfth-century German prioress, writer, artist, and natural healer, was a model of a strong, powerful woman. The words of Meister Eckhart, a medieval theologian and philospher, also inspire me. From the Muslim mystical tradition come the Sufis, perhaps the best known in the West being Rumi.

And there are modern-day mystics, many of whom I have been lucky enough to meet through my work as a writer and editor: Vietnamese Buddhist monk Thich Nhat Hanh, the late teacher Wayne Teasdale, author Joyce Rupp. What all these people—past and present—share is a deep, abiding attention to their inner lives, to the movement of God in their world and the larger world, and to the powerful, yet subtle, voice of the Divine guiding them through it all.

Not all of us can abandon the practical necessities of life to become full-time mystics. But we can learn from those who have. Maybe if we did, we wouldn't be so shaken by the mystery of life.

❡

God, help me to just be with the mysterious parts of life.
And thank you for mystical teachers who help me to do that.

Images of God

Do not think about what will happen tomorrow,
for the same eternal Father who takes care of you today
will look out for you tomorrow and always.
Either he will keep you from evil
or he will give you invincible courage to endure it.

St. Francis de Sales

ᘓᕯ

God must be tired of hearing, "Why me?" Nearly every human being throughout history must have, at some point in their lives, stormed the heavens demanding to know why they have been singled out for suffering. "Why didn't I get the job?" "Why did my wife die?" "Why doesn't he love me?" "Why did the tornado hit my house?" "Why can't I have children?"

These questions, it seems to me, are responses to the seeming unfairness in life. "Why do these things happen to me, *and not to other people?*" Of course, they do happen to others and that is the first step toward recognizing that our pain is not unique and eventually moving toward compassion.

It is true, however, that life can be unfair, and in the midst of pain, God seems like a good target to blame for that unfairness. But I'm not sure God is responsible for all the suffering here on earth, and on top of that I'm also not sure there's all that much that God can do it about it, except to comfort us and help us find some meaning in it.

Some people imagine God as an all-powerful favor-distributor in the sky: If you do what you believe God wants you to, then God will reward you with a pain-free, happy life. While this may work for some people, it doesn't explain why "bad things happen to good people," as the title of a bestselling book put it. Others believe that pain-free happiness comes only after death and so accept suffering as their lot in life, or that it is somehow a purification before everlasting life—a masochistic faith, that one.

Perhaps that's why the image of God as a loving parent persists in Christianity. Parents wish they could protect their children from suffering, but since they can't, moms and dads do their best to kiss their children's boo-boos, reassure them that everything will be all right, and love them through their pain. God as a loving Father or Mother may not be able to answer all our "Why me?" questions, but that image of God can help us feel a little better.

C ◎

God, it is frustrating when I can't understand
why things are happening in my life.
But I turn to you to be with me through it all.

Walking Prayer

So much in life is solved by walking.

St. Augustine

⁓

It is during difficult times in our lives that we most need to turn to God, yet paradoxically it is also during these times that connecting to God through prayer most eludes us. How many times can you pray, "God, please bring me a child"? I have found that when words fail me, other forms of prayer can help: singing, dancing, sitting in silence, praying with your body.

The Christian tradition offers several forms of walking prayer that can help you connect with the Divine when you can't seem to pray with words. One is the labyrinth, an ancient maze-like circle sometimes painted on a floorcloth or created in stone or brick outdoors. The most famous labyrinth is in the floor of the Catholic cathedral in Chartres, France.

Walking the labyrinth involves entering, following the path that twists and turns back and forth, landing in the center, then reversing the twists and turns back to where you began. I have walked it alone and with others, and found both to be powerful. If walked in a prayerful manner, the labyrinth can elicit a number of insights, including the image of life's jagged path that takes us near and then away from our "center," or the need to walk with others on our journey.

I used to walk two miles home from work on a regular basis. Often I would use that time to prayer-walk, repeating a mantra with my measured gait: "God is with me. God is with me." Or I would chant in my head (lest others think I'm crazy) an inspirational song ("Jesus, remember me, when you come into your kingdom"). Today I live too far from work to walk home, but I still use the five blocks from the train to my home to prayer-walk. "My child will come. My child will come. My child will come."

~ ⟋

God, I know I can communicate with you in so many ways. Let my walking be a way of connecting with you.

Psalms

The Lord is my rock, my fortress and my deliverer,
my God, my rock in whom I take refuge.

PSALM 18:2

᠑᠕

If I had to pick a favorite book of the Bible, it would be the book of Psalms in the Hebrew Scriptures. It is a collection of 150 songs—poetry, really—supposedly written by David, the king of the Israelites in 1000 BC, although biblical scholars now believe they were written by several authors and handed down orally until written down in the sixth century BC. The word *psalm* means literally "songs sung to a harp." In the Catholic Mass, we sing a psalm between the first and second readings, and many of those songs have stuck in my memory since childhood.

What I love about the psalms—and why they have been so helpful to me during different times of my life—is the wide range of strong emotion expressed in their words. There are psalms of praise and thanksgiving for when you feel totally blessed by God. "This is the day the Lord has made. Let us rejoice and be glad" (Psalm 118). The psalms of lament really speak to me when life is not going so well: "Insults have broken my heart, so that I am in despair. I looked for pity, but there was none; and for comforters, but I found none" (Psalm 69). There is always an inkling of trust, even when the psalmist feels abandoned: "I lift up my eyes to hills—from where will my help come? My help comes from the Lord, who made heaven and earth" (Psalm 121).

Edmund and I have found that our adoption journey has taken us all over the emotional map. We were ecstatic to choose our initial country and finish our paperwork. Then we were saddened over the lengthening wait, once again happy to see Vietnam as another option, then angry when our second adoption hit every snag imaginable.

If I feel a bit crazy for having all these emotions (sometimes many in one day), I can hum a psalm and remember that throughout human history people have felt the same way. And God has understood.

⟨⟩

God, sometimes it feels like I can't handle all these emotions.
It feels better to get them out in the open.

Mary

Our Lady said yes for the human race.
Each one of us must echo that yes for our lives.
We are all asked if we will surrender what we are,
our humanity, our flesh and blood, to the Holy Spirit
and allow Christ to fill the emptiness
formed by the particular shape of our life.

CARYLL HOUSELANDER

We Catholics love Mary. We worship, respect, and pray to God the Father and Jesus like any Christians, but when times get really tough, who wouldn't turn to a loving mother? Some theologians think Mary functions as a feminine face of God for some people, an image otherwise missing in the Christian tradition. How else could you explain the widespread popularity of Marian devotion, whether to her appearance as Our Lady of Guadalupe for Mexicans, in icons like the Black Madonna or the Sorrowful Mother, or for pilgrims to apparition sites like Lourdes, France, or Medjugorje, Bosnia?

I've always preferred the simple gospel story of Mary, a young woman facing some difficult times in her life. When I became pregnant in college, I believed Mary, another unwed teenage mother, could understand. As my husband and I try to build our family through adoption, I find myself again turning to her. Although not usually seen as an adoptive mother, somehow it seems Mary would understand. Mary never had an easy life, so she easily becomes a patron for anyone going through difficulty.

The thing about Mary is that she never lost faith, and she believed God was with her through it all. Mary was human, so I'm sure she had her bad days, but what is remembered about her is her openness to saying "yes" when faced with an unexplainable pregnancy, her devotion to her family, and finally her fidelity to her son as she waited at the foot of the cross. One of the most powerful pieces of art has to be Michelangelo's *Pieta*, in which a sorrowing Mary holds the body of her crucified son.

Mary knew grief and loss were a part of life, yet she embraced her life with a trust in God that women and men have tried to follow for centuries. Full of grace, indeed.

℮ ☉

Mary, as a woman you understand the pain—and joys—
mothers and mothers-to-be go through.
Be with me on this journey.

St. Joseph

Listen to your own truth,
not to what others say is right or wrong.
Follow your heart; lean on your own inner compass.
Feel the fear, and do it anyway.
Trust that there is a part of you that knows the way.

MARY RUTH BROZ, RSM, AND BARBARA FLYNN

ᏘᎧᏘ

Catholics have patron saints for nearly everything. St. Francis is supposed to help gardeners. Lawyers can pray to St. Thomas More, while journalists have St. Francis de Sales. A few years ago the Vatican even named a patron saint of the Internet: St. Isidore of Seville. And there is an official patron saint for adoptive parents: St. Joseph. According to Catholic teaching on the virgin birth, Mary, Jesus' mother, became pregnant miraculously by God, so Joseph, her husband, is really Jesus' "adoptive" father.

Whether you believe that or not, it can be helpful to have someone in scripture who models the importance of raising someone else's biological child. The problem is that we don't know much about Joseph. He is a minor player in the story, so the Bible doesn't say much about him. What we do know is that he apparently loved Mary very much and stuck by her when things got tough. Scripture scholars also believe he might have been older when Jesus was born (many adoptive parents can relate to that) and probably was dead by the time Jesus began his public ministry.

But as is often the case when we don't have a lot of historical information on a person of faith, we "fill in" with details that seem to make sense to us. Traditional stories about Joseph portray him as a hard-working carpenter who was a perfect father to the young Jesus. But what I've always taken from Joseph's story is the way he trusted his visions, both when an "angel" (which some think is gospel-speak for any way God speaks to you) told him to wed Mary and warned him to escape to Egypt so Jesus would not be killed by Herod.

There have been several times when I have second-guessed some aspect of our adoption process. Did we choose the right agency, the right country? Should we have adopted domestically? Is this worth it? My gut continues to tell me I'm doing the right thing. Thanks to Joseph, I'm going to trust that vision.

God, I believe you speak to me through my gut feelings
that we are pursuing the right thing with these adoptions.
Thank you for providing an example of someone from history
who trusted his visions.

Women in Scripture

Where you go, I will go; where you lodge, I will lodge;
your people shall be my people, and your God my God.

RUTH 1:16

❧

Girl names are so much easier than boy names. This is the consensus of all my friends, at least, and it certainly was true for us. I had dreamed of the name Sophie long before it became as popular as it is now, and my husband readily agreed. But coming up with a name for our son was a lot harder. I wanted something creative and meaningful, but my husband leaned toward tried-and-traditional names.

One day, while perusing one of those baby name websites, we came across Samuel and both liked it. And the two names slip off the tongue easily: "Sam and Sophie, get here right now!" The final kicker was that Samuel means "God heard." In the Hebrew Scriptures, Samuel is born to Hannah after years of infertility.

Hannah isn't the only "barren" woman in the Christian and Hebrew Scriptures. There are Sarah, Rebekah, Rachel and Elizabeth to name a few. You'd think these women would provide comfort and inspiration to contemporary infertile women—and perhaps they do for some. They didn't for me.

First of all, in the patriarchal cultures of biblical times, the woman was always blamed for infertility, which as we now know is only true about half the time when couples can't conceive. And too often the biblical woman's infertility is portrayed as a punishment from God, and the eventual child as God finally sending a miracle—an outcome that may not happen for many of us.

Biblical scholars point out that infertility is not the point of these stories. It's not about either the mother's or the father's inability to bear children; it's about the child. And a child born as the result of a miracle is a sign that the child will not be an ordinary person.

That is not to say that these women in scripture can't inspire us. I have found a great deal of comfort in the story of Elizabeth, Mary's cousin, and her friendship with Mary, as they both went through crooked paths to build their families. Women have always stuck together.

⟶ ⟵

God, thank you for the women who inspire me—
both women from scripture
and those who walk my crooked path with me today.

Worshiping in Community

We have all known the long loneliness
and we have learned that the only solution is love
and that love comes in community.

DOROTHY DAY

֍

Several times a year our parish gathers nearly everyone together for one Mass. I love how full the church is, the voices strong in song, and the energy contagious. This year, at one such all-parish Mass on Pentecost, our pastor preached about places in our parish where he sees the Spirit at work. One of those places he named was in adoptive families.

Our parish, St. Gertrude in Chicago, is rather unique. It is a haven for progressive Catholics, yet still populated by little old ladies who have lived in the neighborhood for decades. Newcomers include yuppies and African immigrants. There are a number of gay and lesbian families, and social justice and equality play an important role in the minds of most parishioners. Many of them have adopted transracially and internationally, making adoption a very visible reality to anyone who attends the ten o'clock family Mass.

Not everyone is lucky enough to have a parish that values adoption as much as ours. But a growing number are starting adoption support groups. And some priests and ministers, thanks to visible adoptive families, are becoming more sensitive to the reality that there is more than one way to build a family.

Edmund and I can think of a dozen reasons to skip Mass most Sunday mornings, chief among them our need and desire for more sleep. But while it was hard to see all the babies and families at church, we knew that we needed to be in a spiritual community for our faith to hold. As important as our personal relationship with

God is, we need a family of faith—other people around us who are trying to live the gospel—to make it through the hard times in our lives. They will also be there to celebrate our good news with us.

God, thank you for the faith community
that has nurtured us during this wait.
Help us to be that community
for others in their struggles too.

Silence

There are times when silence has the loudest voice.

LEROY BROWNLOW

ᐁᘓ

When I was separated from my first husband, I stopped going to church because I couldn't stand to be alone with my thoughts for a whole hour. At home I fell asleep with the television on and I kept myself busy during the day with work, friends, and other activities. Silence was the enemy.

Once I got through that ultra-painful period, silence wasn't so scary. Ultimately I learned that silence is where I hear what my heart is really telling me—what I believe to be God's voice. As an off-the-Myers-Briggs-chart extrovert, I also can verbalize my way into understanding my heart's desires, and I have heard the voice of the Divine speak to me through friends and other people. But I still need silence to get grounded so those conversations will be meaningful and fruitful.

Are Edmund and I doing the right thing? Does God want us to be parents? Am I going to make it through this process? I believe the answers to these questions can be found in silence.

Silence is hard to cultivate in today's world. I wake up to the voice of Renee Montagne on NPR and listen to Stephen Colbert before I drift off to sleep. But I can catch snippets of silence on the train to work (if I'm not sitting near someone on a cell phone), and even my walk to and from the train can offer five minutes of quiet time.

A co-worker went on a week-long silent retreat. I've always been intrigued by such a thing, because I didn't think I could survive it. I know when my home is shared with two boisterous toddlers, a silent retreat will seem like a dream. Let us try to cultivate silence now.

❧

God, I hear your voice in silence.
Help me to cultivate regular periods of quiet so I can hear it.

Miracles

God always finishes his sentences.

ALBERT PAYSON TERHUNE

⌒⌒

"You're adopting?" the woman I'd just met at the conference exclaimed. "Then you'll love this story." She went on to tell how her sister had been trying to adopt domestically and was not having any luck. So this woman went to Fatima, a pilgrimage site where Mary is said to have appeared, and had a vision that her sister was going to get her child soon. She returned home and told her sister to get the baby's room ready. And, sure enough, within weeks she had adopted a newborn.

Some people find those kinds of stories hopeful, imagining that their miracle is just around the corner. If your world is in chaos, it can be helpful to believe in a God who is somehow in charge, a benevolent grandfather in the sky who will grant your every wish if you just pray hard enough and be good.

Before I began infertility treatments, I was traveling in India and visited the grave of Mother Teresa. Knowing that she is on the path to sainthood, I prayed there to become pregnant, thinking if I did, my miracle might help her canonization cause. It never happened.

"That's a nice story," I told the woman at the conference. "But I'm not sure how that's helpful to me." Then I explained how I have prayed very hard myself, and many of my friends and family have too. "Does God like your sister better? Does God think I shouldn't be a mother?" If I believe in a God who doles out miracles, then either I am a second-class person who doesn't deserve one, or God is a big meannie.

The poor woman slinked away from me. She was only trying to be kind, and I'm sure my outburst did not change her theology one iota.

But neither do stories of such "miracles" change mine. I don't believe God controls whether or not I get pregnant or have a child, but God is still powerful. In fact, I feel God's presence even more clearly when I am hurting.

God is with me in my pain, not causing it. And God is with me in my joy. That, to me, is the real miracle.

℃ ☺

God, be with me as I struggle during this wait.
Give me the vision to see the miracle in the process
and in the face of my child.

EPILOGUE

∽

"It will be so worth it." That's what every single adoptive parent said to Edmund and me while we were waiting for our children. My head knew they were right, but some days my bruised heart just couldn't believe it. Yes, we would probably agree that the wait was worth it once we had our child—the key phrase being *once we had our child*.

Then one sunny May day, after several weeks of being told by our agency that "any day now" we would get our referral that matched us with our son, I woke up and decided to finish some errands on the computer that I had been putting off, chief among them making donations for recent disasters, including the devastating earthquake in China.

Minutes after clicking "donate" on a few websites, I got an email from our adoption coordinator asking if Edmund and I were available that morning. I called her immediately: "Ed is at school doing his student teaching, but he could come home if this is it." Her response: "He better come home."

That day we received the news that a seven-month-old boy in an orphanage in Ho Chi Minh City had been officially matched with us. His given name was "Dieu"—which means "wonderful and gentle" in Vietnamese but also "God" in French. We knew whom to thank for this wonderful news.

But our wait wasn't over yet.

Allegations of fraud and trafficking had led to an end of adoptions between the United States and Vietnam. Those with a referral before September 1 would be allowed to complete their adoptions, although the U.S. government was scrutinizing each visa application and requiring pre-approval before travel, adding additional wait time.

Our joy was tempered with caution. It wasn't official until the

U.S. government gave us that pre-approval, but we couldn't help but fall in love with the photos and video of arguably the world's most adorable baby. Still, as the weeks wore on, we grew depressed. Now that we knew who this little person was, it would be even more devastating if it didn't work out.

Our case hit a few snags, adding additional stress. I cancelled a baby shower because I was afraid I couldn't act happy when I was still so nervous about whether we would be allowed to adopt this child. What if our referral fell through after the September 1 deadline? I refused to even ask that question out loud.

In early September I once again sat down with a list of errands that had been piling up, including writing some long overdue checks as wedding and graduation gifts for family members.

The next morning we got the call: "Time to go to Vietnam. You've been approved." Seven days later we landed in Ho Chi Minh City and the day after that we met our son, Samuel Dieu, for the first time.

To say that it has been the most joyful experience of our lives would be a massive understatement. Every day we look at each other and say, "We are so lucky to have this child as our son." Seriously—every day. It's almost a bit gaggy.

Looking back at how it all unfolded, I was struck by the coincidence that our two good news calls came after I had intentionally focused on others who were hurting or celebrating. It was a reminder to me that our problems, or our joys, are not the only thing going on in the world, even though it may feel like that at times.

Of course, we can't imagine having any other child but this one as our son. And it wouldn't be this child if our wait had been significantly shorter. In the end, the timing was exactly right, despite all of our crying and complaining that it was all wrong. Once again, Edmund and I learned that when life seems to be falling apart, we must trust that good will come out of it. Life always triumphs over death—that is the heart of the Christian message.

We also learned to lean on each other during the hard times and to seek support from family, friends, and faith throughout this process. I won't say it was easy, but yes, it was so worth it.

Also Available from ACTA Publications

LITTLE LUCY'S FAMILY
A Story About Adoption
Eleanor Gormally
This whimsically-illustrated children's picture book tells the story of how Lucy's adoptive parents traveled to Russia to adopt her, how they brought her home, and how they ultimately became a happy family. The message is universal and can be used for children adopted from any foreign country.
36-page paperback, $14.95

PRAYERS FOR SLEEPLESS NIGHTS
Helen Reichert Lambin
A touching collection of reflections and prayers for the many sources of stress and tension that keep us up late at night.
80-page leatherette cover, $12.95

THE BOOK OF CATHOLIC JOKES
Tom Sheridan
Religion is far too important to be taken seriously all the time, so says author Tom Sheridan. He invites readers to laugh along with him and remember that faith can be—and should be—fun.
128-page paperback, $10.95

RUNNING INTO THE ARMS OF GOD
Patrick Hannon, CSC
Twenty-one stories of prayer by one of the finest Catholic storytellers.
128-page hardcover, $17.95, paperback, $12.95

STORIES
John Shea
Thirty-five of John Shea's favorite and best-known short stories are collected here for the first time in a gorgeous, leatherette-bound volume.
304-page leatherette cover, $14.95

Available from booksellers
or visit www.actapublications.com.